Resources for Teaching French 14–16

Also available from Continuum

Resources for Teaching Mathematics: 14–16, Colin Foster
Resources for Teaching History: 11–14, Susie Hodge
Resources for Teaching History: 14–16, Susie Hodge
Resources for Teaching Creative Writing, Johnnie Young
Resources for Teaching English: 11–14, Helena Ceranic
Resources for Teaching English: 14–16, David A. Hill

Resources for Teaching French 14–16

Gill James

Teachers' resources to accompany this book are available online at:
http://education.james.continuumbooks.com

Please visit the link and register with us to receive your password and to access these downloadable resources.

If you experience any problems accessing the resources, please contact Continuum at:
info@continuumbooks.com

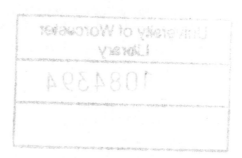

continuum

Continuum International Publishing Group

The Tower Building   Suite 704
11 York Road   80 Maiden Lane
London   New York
SE1 7NX   NY 10038

www.continuumbooks.com

© Gill James 2010

British Library Cataloguing-in-Publication Data
A catalogue record for this book is available from the British Library.

ISBN: 9780826409928 (pb)

Library of Congress Cataloging-in-Publication Data
James, Gill.
Resources for teaching French / Gill James.
     p. cm.
Includes bibliographical references.
ISBN 978-0-8264-0992-8 (paperback)
1. French language   Study and teaching (Secondary)—English speakers.
I. Title.

PC2066.J36 2010   448.071'2—dc22

Typeset by Pindar NZ, Auckland, New Zealand
Printed and bound in Great Britain by Bell & Bain Ltd, Glasgow.

Mixed Sources
Product group from well-managed forests and other controlled sources
www.fsc.org   Cert no. TT-COC-002769
© 1996 Forest Stewardship Council

Contents

Notes for Teachers

How to use this resource

It is a good idea before you start using this resource to read it from cover to cover as if it were a teaching guide. Thereafter, the resource can be dipped into as the teacher wishes, though it would be wise to use the lesson plans within each skill in the order suggested on p. x. The lessons can be adapted for most age groups though it is ideal to start in the final term of Year 9 (ages 14–15).

The ideas presented here have a distinct fundamental methodology based on student motivation. For the lessons outlined to work, the students must take responsibility for their learning and the teacher must be of the opinion that they are able to do so.

The following long-term strategies will enhance the effectiveness of this course:

- Using Tandem Learning, where your student is linked with a French-speaking learner of English. The two students negotiate how they may help each other, working half the time in English and half the time in French; half the time on your student's needs and half the time on the French speaker's needs.

- Setting up banks of materials for reading and listening that students can easily access. Consider using either a library system or make them downloadable from a members-only part of your school website.

- Recording notes from discussions with students in a retrievable form – via a computer or an interactive whiteboard.

- Integrating work with your language assistant into the lessons and making him/her fully aware of the fundamental principles behind the course.

It is advised that you give some thought to these strategies well in advance of the course.

The Companion website

The Continuum Companion website offers copies of the student sheets online, the audio files, transcripts of the audio files and answers to the questions for reading and listening activities. The teacher will therefore be able to display these items via a data projector, an interactive whiteboard or on individual computer screens. See *http://education.james.continuumbooks.com*

Lesson plans

Each lesson plan:

- gives advice about the aims and outcomes of the lesson
- lists the materials needed
- suggests how to group students and how to set up the classroom for each lesson
- breaks each part of the lesson down into approximate categories (lesson starter, main lesson, plenary) with suggested time slots
- provides a Teacher's sheet and photocopiable (and downloadable) Student Sheet
- is designed to be one hour long
- includes suggested homework ideas/activities
- offers 'To make it harder' and 'To make it easier' sections for different abilty students.

The way students are grouped has been carefully considered since the dynamics have been designed to optimize the learning in each lesson. Generally, if mixed-ability is suggested, the recommendation is to mix high with middle and middle with high or lower. Even if friendship groups are allowed, try to mix personalities and gender.

Similar lessons have been clustered together in this resource – for example, language awareness lessons, language habits and practice in the skills, though a teacher using the resource will probably not wish to work through one skill at a time. A route through, which gives a balance of different skills, is suggested below on p. x.

The lesson plans can be mixed and matched to suit individual class needs, provided each subset is completed in order. The 'reminders' at the end of each Student Sheet work well with this path. If a different route is followed, these may need to be adjusted.

Not all of the student sheets contain instructions so the teacher must always explain the activity clearly before they distribute them.

Work with native speakers

There is great emphasis in each lesson plan about how you might involve your language assistant and indeed any other contact with native speakers of French such as your students' exchange partners or penfriend and people they might meet on a trip to a country where French is spoken.

Underlying principles

The two main principles of the course are that the students should acquire language-learning habits and that they should take responsibility for their own learning. This means that they see why the habit is necessary and then they adapt it to the extent that they begin automatically to use that habit and cease to notice that they are working on their language. Time management should no longer be an issue if they take these principles on board.

Online and other resources

Most of the lesson plans refer to other resources you may find useful. Some are from other publishers. Many of them are online and absolutely free of charge. These resources contain a mixture of materials for native speakers of French and for learners of French.

Integration of this resource with your own resources

This resource is particularly designed for use with students aged 14–16. It can and should be used in conjunction with other materials, already in school, and this resource may indeed not be the main component of your course.

Although all the examples in this course relate to French, the skills learned by any student who has followed the course can be applied to other languages. Followed to the letter and in the spirit, these lessons can take students way beyond their own and your own expectations.

Author's note: where the following texts refer to 'she', this is shorthand for either 'she' or 'he' – this is used to avoid clumsy locutions.

A suggested route through:

Getting the Big Picture
1 2 3

Language Learning Habits
4 5 6 7 8 9

Main body
10 23 32 42 48 54
11 24 33 43 49 55
12 23 34 44 50 56
13 26 35 45 51 57
14 27 36 46 52 58
15 28 37 47 53 59
16 29 38 60
17 30 39 61
18 31 40 62
19 41 63

Presentations
20 21 23

Revision and Diagnositcs
64 74
65 75
66 76
67 77
68 78
69 79
80

Exam
70 71 72 73

Lesson Plans

This resource is designed to be flexible, so you can dip in and out of it as you please. However, if you follow the lesson plans in the order suggested below (1 to 4, followed by 10, and so on), students will be exposed to a balance of lesson types in a logical order. They will progress through language awareness, language habit, language skill and revision lessons.

Getting the Big Picture	1 ◆ Why do we learn languages?	2 ◆ What is involved in learning a language?	3 ◆ What are my strengths and weaknesses?										
Language Learning Habits	4 ◆ What are my tools?	5 ◆ How will I organise my work?	6 ◆ How can I find time for language learning?	7 ◆ Which resources do I have to help me with my learning?	8 ◆ Working with an exchange partner	9 ◆ Making the most of a trip to France							
Speaking	10 ◆ Role Play 1	11 ◆ Role Play 2 – General Phrases	12 ◆ Role Play 3 – Adapting the Role Play	13 ◆ Role Play 4 – Extending the Role Play	14 ◆ Role Play 5 – Mastering All Role Plays	15 ◆ Personal Questions 1	16 ◆ Personal questions 2	17 ◆ Personal questions 3 – Extending and Enhancing Your Answers	18 ◆ Personal questions 4 – Really Showing Off	19 ◆ Topic Presentations 1 – Preparing the Presentation	20 ◆ Topic Presentations 2 – Rehearsing the Presentation	21 ◆ Topic Presentations 3 – Extending the Presentation through Questions	22 ◆ Topic Presentations 4 – Celebration and Evaluation
Listening	23 ◆ Listening Situations	24 ◆ Decoding What You Hear	25 ◆ Tackling the Questions	26 ◆ Listening Exercise 1	27 ◆ Listening Exercise 2	28 ◆ Listening Exercise 3	29 ◆ Listening Exercise 4	30 ◆ Listening Exercise 5	31 ◆ How to Work on your Listening				
Reading	32 ◆ An Introduction to Intensive Reading	33 ◆ Dealing with Questions	34 ◆ Intensive Reading and Building Sentences	35 ◆ Intensive Reading and Building Questions	36 ◆ Intensive Reading – How to Practice Effectively	37 ◆ Extensive Reading – An Introduction	38 ◆ Extensive Reading – An adventure on the web	39 ◆ Extensive Reading – Reading for pleasure	40 ◆ Extensive Reading – Reading for information	41 ◆ Extensive Reading – Making the most of your opportunities			
Writing	42 ◆ Open-ended Questions	43 ◆ Cloning and Adapting	44 ◆ Writing with Patterns	45 ◆ Writing with the Sentences	46 ◆ Editing Your Work	47 ◆ Reacting to Marked Work							
Vocabulary Building	48 ◆ Collecting Words	49 ◆ Dictionary Skills	50 ◆ Colour Haikus	51 ◆ Acrostic Poems	52 ◆ Creative Exchange with a Native Speaker	53 ◆ Walking with your Eyes Open							
Grammar Building	54 ◆ A Grammar Overview	55 ◆ Verbs – Tenses	56 ◆ Verbs – Person	57 ◆ Verbs – Voice	58 ◆ Verbs – Mood	59 ◆ Word Order	60 ◆ Prepositions	61 ◆ Parts of Speech	62 ◆ Gender and Number	63 ◆ Numbers, Times and Quantities			
Revision	64 ◆ General Overview	65 ◆ Planning how to Revise	66 ◆ Revising for the Oral Exam	67 ◆ Revising for the Listening Exam	68 ◆ Revising for the Reading Exam	69 ◆ Revising for the Writing Exam							
The Exam	70 ◆ The Oral Exam	71 ◆ The Listening Exam	72 ◆ The Reading Exam	73 ◆ The Writing Exam									
Diagnostics	74 ◆ Vocabulary	75 ◆ Grammar	76 ◆ Listening	77 ◆ Speaking	78 ◆ Reading	79 ◆ Writing	80 ◆ Revisiting the Big Picture						

Getting the Big Picture

Aims and outcomes

To enable students to understand why they are learning French.

Materials needed

- Student Sheet 1
- interactive whiteboard
- large (A3) pieces of paper
- coloured pens

Classroom setup

Put students into groups of three to five. You can use friendship groups on this occasion.

Lesson starter (10 minutes)

Why do we learn languages?

Discuss this question with your students. Build a mindmap on the board with 'Learning French' in the middle (look at the Mindmap on Student Sheet 2 for information). The first ring around the mindmap should include all the reasons students can think of. They may include some French-specific ideas.

When you have got a dozen or so reasons, draw further links from each reason, showing what further advantages there might be because of that reason.

You may come across the following suggestions:

1. Other people learn English – we ought to learn their language. *If other people have learnt our language and we have not learnt theirs, they have had an experience we haven't had. We may be missing out on something.*

2. Some courses need languages. *Why has someone decided it is important? Talk to the students about skills they acquire in learning languages they might use elsewhere. For instance, people good at languages often make good programmers.*

3. Some jobs need languages. *There are obvious ones, of course, but do remember to point out less obvious ones, such as publishing and Information Technology (IT).*

Main lesson (35 minutes)

Each group should produce their own mindmap, using large sheets of paper and coloured pens. Ask each group to appoint a scribe and a spokesperson. Try to spend a little time with each group. Allow students 20 minutes for this task.

Allow each group to give feedback to the rest of the class (15 minutes). Create a new mindmap as you go along. They need only add anything new from the shared feedback.

Plenary (10 minutes)

Give the whole class some general feedback.

Homework (5 minutes)

Students are to create their own mindmaps about why they want to study French. The prompts provided on the Student Sheet provided will guide them through this. It is a good idea to discuss these in a subsequent lesson and also take them in to 'mark'. Students will appreciate your comments on their work.

To make it harder

Students may need to go on to another piece of paper for this.

For each specific thing they would like to be able to do, the students should write a list of what they can already do. They may not think that there is much they can do yet, but they should put down even the smallest thing. Then they should write a list of what they definitely cannot do yet and what they think is essential to enable them to do what they think they need to do.

Now they have a list of all the aspects of French they need to polish up and all the aspects of French that they have to learn. Is that their work for the next two years? Where might they find some help with this?

To make it easier

Student should simply make a list of all the areas that they think they need to cover.

FURTHER RESOURCES

There are several links to sites that give lots of information about mindmaps and about learning languages in the online resources (for the web address please see p. iii).

Create your own mindmap about why you want or need to learn a language.

Draw a circle in the middle of an A4 piece of paper (landscape) and in the centre write 'Why I need to learn French'.

Write down as many reasons as you can think of. Some may be to do with the advantages of learning a language; some may be specifically to do with learning French. It is fine to include 'get another GCSE', but try to put down why a language GCSE, or better still, why one in French specifically, is important.

Look at each reason you have picked. Continuing with your mindmap, for each reason write down four or five specific things that you would like to be able to do. For example, if you have said that you would like to live in France some time, list some of the activities you will need your French for: understanding the television, going shopping, understanding at work, being able to make yourself understood when you go out with friends, making friends.

✻ Reminder: Learning a language can help you communicate with people from different countries.

Aims and outcomes

To enable the student to understand what components are involved in language learning.

Materials needed

- Student Sheet 2
- interactive whiteboard
- coloured pens and paper

Classroom setup

Let the students work in groups of four or five. Form the groups in a different way from previous lessons.

Lesson starter (10 minutes)

Discuss with students what they think is involved in learning a language. List some of their ideas.

Main lesson (20 minutes)

Let the students work in groups of four or five. They should produce a mindmap, which may look something like the one on Student Sheet 1.

Plenary (20 minutes)

Hold a plenary session and create a large mindmap that brings together all the ideas from all the groups.

Give out the Student Sheets and explain any of the terms the students have not met. They may well need some explanation of all the grammatical terms and you may need to explain that grammar is what makes a language more than a collection of words. For example, you could say that grammar is the backbone of a language: if you master grammar you can take charge of the language and build up anything you like.

You may also find it useful to look forward yourself to later lessons on writing, the difference between active and passive skills and the sections on grammar.

It would be useful also to have some discussion of why it is necessary to acquire language-learning habits: a short answer is that language learning then becomes second nature, since you will be doing things, such as reading in your new language, that help you to learn and it won't feel like work because you'll be having fun.

Homework (10 minutes)

Students to complete Student Sheet 2. Make sure they understand the instructions on the sheet. Make time to discuss the homework the next time you meet. Again, taking in the work may be a good idea.

To make it harder

Ask the students to conduct an internet search to look for more ideas about language learning.

To make it easier

Ask the students to compile a list of three items they understand well and three items they understand less well.

FURTHER RESOURCES

Gill James, *The Complete Guide to Learning a Language* (How to Books Ltd., 2003), has explanations for adult learners of many of the terms in this course.

http://french.about.com/od/grammar/French_Grammar.htm has some interesting explanations for teachers.

www.realfrench.net/index.php has some interesting exercises for students.

Study the mindmap.

Add in anything you or your classmates may have thought of earlier when you were talking about it with your teacher.

Now work with different coloured highlighters. Use one colour to highlight all those things you understand well.

Then spend about twenty minutes looking through whatever resources you have at home – your own notes, your textbooks, any dictionary you may own, the internet. Use a different colour for what you may now understand better after using these.

Finally, use a third colour for those things that you still find puzzling.

You will be able to use this as a basis for a discussion next lesson.

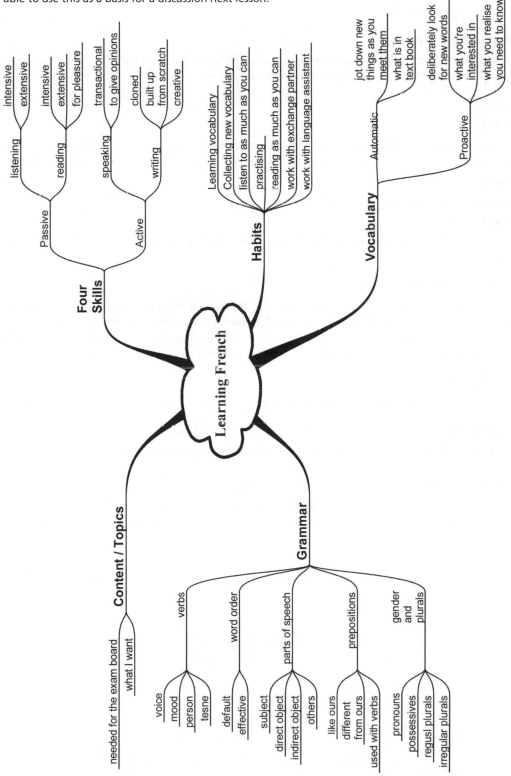

✳ Reminder: Working with mind maps is useful.

Aims and outcomes

To enable students to understand their own strengths and weaknesses and make an appropriate action plan.

Materials needed

- Student Sheet 3
- homework from Lesson 2
- interactive whiteboard

Classroom setup

Students should work in pairs.

Lesson starter (10 minutes)

Discuss with students what they found out from the homework. Keep a list on the board of what people know well, what they know less well and what they have managed to find a bit more information about.

Main lesson

(10 minutes)

Discuss with the students where they might get help with some of these topics. A likely answer might be: wall displays in the classroom, textbooks, their own notes, the language assistant, the teacher, their parents, a native speaker, the internet.

(10 minutes)

Clarify some of the items commonly not understood.

(20 minutes)

Give out the Student Sheets and ask them to fill them in. If they finish quickly, they can discuss their answers with the person sitting next to them.

Homework (10 minutes)

Students are to make an action plan based on their answers. Be careful that the students are not overwhelmed by what needs to be done. Discuss how they should decide on three actions that will make the most difference, and then decide how often they should do this. Encourage them to be very specific and realistic in what they plan to do. Emphasize that this is a plan that they should revisit every so often. It may be useful to have extra copies available.

To make it harder

Ask the students to define more closely in which ways they are good or less good at some aspects of learning French.

To make it easier

Ask the students to list three areas they are very good at and three areas where they need to do a lot of work.

FURTHER RESOURCES

www.kent.ac.uk/careers/sk/skillsactionplanning.htm contains some useful tips on action planning.

www.language-learning-tips.com/02_forming_positive_habits.htm discusses some language learning habits.

http://entertainment.timesonline.co.uk/tol/arts_and_entertainment/books/book_extracts/article773282.ece is an interesting article about language learning habits.

www4.ncsu.edu/~fljpm/clinic/sj11.study.html gives some tips about getting organized to study.

Study the table below. Mark with a tick where you are placed for each of these skills and/or areas of knowledge.

Skill / Knowledge Area	I am really good at this.	I am quite good at this.	I need to do some more work on this.	I need to do a lot more work on this.
The exam content				
What I want to know				
Listening				
Speaking				
Reading				
Writing				
Vocabulary known				
Collecting new vocabulary				
Learning new vocabulary				
Reading on my own				
Working with my exchange partner				
Working with the language assistant				
Verbs				
Word order				
Prepositions				
Parts of speech				
Number and gender				

There is a blank row at the bottom of the table for you to add in any other areas you can think of. Can you find three areas you could improve which will make a big difference? Make an action plan for these areas.

✳ **Reminder: You can have control over your learning.**

What are my Strengths and Weaknesses? **STUDENT SHEET 3**

Language Learning Habits

Aims and outcomes

To familiarize the students with all the tools they need for language learning. Students will be asked to design their own lessons.

Materials needed

- Student Sheet 4, photocopied and cut into strips, so that each student gets one of the Designer Lesson instruction sheets.
- a beautifully decorated classroom; set the classroom out a little like a marketplace, with five tables or areas set with:
  - hardware and any CDs or other resources used with the course
  - various textbooks
  - a computer (or computers, depending on space)
  - some of the students' own notebooks and exercise books, and perhaps some borrowed from more advanced students
  - a selection of dictionaries on the final table
  - paper and pens for feedback sessions

Classroom setup

Before the students arrive, sort them into four groups. Mixed-ability groups works well for this lesson. Mix average children with either weaker or more able ones. Direct each student to a table as they arrive. Place a set of instuctions on each table, so one group of students is making a lesson plan about the family, another about hobbies, another about where they live, another about holidays and the final group about school.

Lesson starter

(10 minutes)

Give a quick 'tour' of what is on offer. Point out classroom displays. Show the students what the hardware can do. Show them the textbooks. Point out the different sections – contents, index, vocabulary and grammar sections. Show them a few resources you have on the computer and some resources you know of on the internet. Show them the various dictionaries. Encourage them to own one themselves. If you have a language assistant, ask them to tell the students the ways in which they might be able to help.

(5 minutes)

Set the five 'Designer Lesson' tasks described on the Student Sheet. You might like to display this on the interactive whiteboard or print it off and cut it up. Each group does one. They need to think of how a perfect lesson might be put together. They can move to other areas to look at the tools. They can even take them over to their tables, but must return them. Remind them they will have to appoint a scribe and a spokesperson. Expect some chaos!

Main lesson (35 minutes)

Allow students to plan their own 'Designer Lessons' according to the instructions on Student Sheet 4.

Remind students to complete and write up their 'Designer Lesson' plan.

Plenary (10 minutes)

Groups describe their lesson to other groups. Question them about why they have selected particular tools.

Homework (5 minutes)

Ask the students to design their own perfect lesson on any topic they like.

To make it harder

Ask the students to have a go at being the teacher next lesson and taking the class through the lesson they have prepared.

To make it easier

Students may make a list of five useful activities without worrying about lesson times.

Make your own Designer Lesson.

Your turn to be the teacher

Use all the resources you have been shown by the teacher to design a perfect lesson – and homework if you wish. Remember to use classroom displays, any hardware, resources on the computer and the internet, the language assistant, your own notes, dictionaries and any textbooks that are available. Think of the advantages and disadvantages of using each tool. Try to get a little each of listening, reading, speaking and writing into your lesson. Have an open-ended task for your students at the end.

Your group's theme: All about my family.

Your turn to be the teacher

Use all the resources you have been shown by the teacher to design a perfect lesson – and homework if you wish. Remember to use classroom displays, any hardware, resources on the computer and the internet, the language assistant, your own notes, dictionaries and any textbooks that are available. Think of the advantages and disadvantages of using each tool. Try to get a little each of listening, reading, speaking and writing into your lesson. Have an open-ended task for your students at the end.

Your group's theme: All about my hobbies.

Your turn to be the teacher

Use all of the resources you have been shown by the teacher to design a perfect lesson – and homework if you wish. Remember to use classroom displays, any hardware, resources on the computer and the internet, the language assistant, your own notes, dictionaries and any textbooks that are available. Think of the advantages and disadvantages of using each tool. Try to get a little each of listening, reading, speaking and writing into your lesson. Have an open-ended task for your students at the end.

Your group's theme: All about where I live.

Your turn to be the teacher

Use all of the resources you have been shown by the teacher to design a perfect lesson – and homework if you wish. Remember to use classroom displays, any hardware, resources on the computer and the internet, the language assistant, your own notes, dictionaries and any textbooks that are available. Think of the advantages and disadvantages of using each tool. Try to get a little each of listening, reading, speaking and writing into your lesson. Have an open-ended task for your students at the end.

Your group's theme: All about my holidays.

Your turn to be the teacher

Use all of the resources you have been shown by the teacher to design a perfect lesson – and homework if you wish. Remember to use classroom displays, any hardware, resources on the computer and the internet, the language assistant, your own notes, dictionaries and any textbooks that are available. Think of the advantages and disadvantages of using each tool. Try to get a little each of listening, reading, speaking and writing into your lesson. Have an open-ended task for your students at the end.

Your group's theme: All about my school

✳ Reminder: Why do we learn languages?

Aims and outcomes

To enable the students to find a way of organizing their work that will suit them.

Materials needed

- Student Sheet 5
- all the stationery you can find
- copies of the office catalogue that you order supplies from (you might even like to have some catalogues from a High Street store or from the internet)
- students should bring any work they have (it might be useful to have some work from more advanced students available)
- interactive whiteboard
- computers

Classroom setup

Students should work in mixed-ability pairs.

Hint

Most teachers already have a fixed idea about how they want students to organize their work. However, you might consider coming to an agreement with the whole group or indeed allowing individual students to do what suits them best.

Lesson starter (15 minutes)

Introduce the students to all the beautiful, exciting stationery that you have or have catalogues about. Also talk about how they might use the computer – for example, for word processing, recording vocabulary and storing an electronic bilingual dictionary. Talk about the advantages and disadvantages of each item.

Point out what type of work they need to store. You might mention and expand on those listed on the Student Sheet. Discuss examples of each type from the collection of student work you have in the room. Discuss the student sheet.

Main lesson (20 minutes)

Allow the students to work in pairs to fill in ideas on the Student Sheet.

Plenary (20 minutes)

Discuss student ideas. Draw out of them the advantages and disadvantages of each retrieval system.

Homework (5 minutes)

Students should start organizing their work. Give them the stationery they need.

To make it harder

Ask the students to present a package of storage materials to the rest of the classs and argue about why these would be ideal.

To make it easier

Ask the students to discuss each type of activity and the stationery available in turn.

FURTHER RESOURCES

These online catalogues give plenty of ideas of what types of stationery is available:

Staples *www.staples.co.uk/ENG/catalog/stap_home.asp?ct=1*

The Consortium *www.theconsortium.com/school-stationery.htm*

Office Shopping *www.officeshopping.co.uk/features/backtoschool.asp*

Hint

If you have the chance to travel to Europe, check out some of the supplies they stock in local supermarkets.

Decide how you would like to organize the following types of work:

Notes

Mindmaps and questionnaires such as this

Handouts containing vital information

Corrected work

Modelled work (oral topic answers, presentations etc.)

'Throw away' (work you do but never refer to again)

Examples on A4 sheets

Vocabulary

Grammar notes

Other

Think carefully about the advantages and disadvantages of each storage system. You may find it helpful to discuss this with a friend.

✳ Reminder: What is involved in learning a language?

How Will I Organize my Work?   **STUDENT SHEET 5**

Aims and outcomes

To enable the students to get into language learning routines and maximize the time they have available for language learning.

Materials needed

- Student Sheet 6
- interactive whiteboard
- a notebook for each student to use as a diary for a week (they may be able to use something they already have, such as a homework diary or organizer)

Classroom setup

Students should work in mixed-ability pairs.

Hint

It may be useful for you as a teacher to go through this process. You might focus on improving your French even more, working on another language you know less well or working on something different altogether.

Lesson starter (12 minutes)

It's like brushing your teeth . . . or playing scales . . . or warming up for football

Identify all those language-learning habits you can do in just a few minutes a day – for example, learning vocabulary, looking over corrected work or practising spoken language with a friend. Put ideas up on the whiteboard. If you can save them, that would be even better.

Allow the students to fill in the first part of their sheet.

Main lesson

(12 minutes)

A little goes a long way

Ask the students to think of ways they can find a few extra minutes for their French, for example, by getting up a little earlier, going to bed a little later, spending one break a week working with a friend on their French, forming a French club, playing a game in French with a friend.

Allow the students to fill in the second part of their sheet.

(12 minutes)

You won't even notice you're doing it after a while

Suggest some leisure activities that can take place in French – surfing the web, listening to music, chatting up members of the opposite sex (!), watching a football match in French, setting a DVD to French – and get them to think of other ideas.

Allow students to fill in the third part of their sheet.

Plenary (12 minutes)

There are some things you just have to do!

Try to identify some activities the students can do that will make a big difference and not take up too much time, for example, finding time each day to practise each of the four skills on Student Sheet 2, and keeping a diary in French which they hand in every so often to be corrected.

Homework (12 minutes)

Students are to look at these sheets daily over the course of a week and decide which of these ideas they can do each day. They should record what they do and how they get on. A feedback lesson should be held later to see how the students have managed this and to try to persuade them to make these habits permanent.

To make it harder

Ask the students to involve parents and siblings in keeping them on track.

To make it easier

The teacher may collect everybody's ideas and make a chart in class. S/he can check with members of the class from time to time to see how they are getting on.

It's like brushing your teeth . . . or playing scales . . . or warming up for football	A little goes a long way
You won't even notice you're doing it after a while	There are some things you just have to do

✳ Reminder: Are you remembering to organize your work properly?

How Can I Find Time for Language Learning?   **STUDENT SHEET 6**

Aims and outcomes

To familiarize your students with all the resources available to them.

Materials needed

- Student Sheet 7
- interactive whiteboard
- examples of all the textbooks students will be using on the course
- dictionaries, extra books and resources you have in your classroom, the department, the Learning Resource Centre and on the computer
- perhaps a live link to your French partner school
- the language assistant, if possible
- consider making this a mobile lesson, including a visit to the Learning Resource Centre
- 'free' materials – 'junk mail' and any internet pages that offer rich learning opportunities for your students (try to make some of these link to the mini-projects described on Student Sheet 7)

Classroom setup

Students work individually in this lesson.

Hint

This lesson revisits to some extent what students learnt in Lesson 4. Part of this lesson can be used for recapping and checking progress.

Lesson starter (15 minutes)

Recap of Lesson 4.

Introduce some of the free materials. Also, start to discuss how useful it might be to work with a native speaker. This will be extended in the next lesson.

Main lesson (30 minutes)

See the Student Sheet. Using the resources you have shown them, they are to complete one of the mini-projects suggested. This will only be rough at this stage and will probably be unfinished.

Allow the students to work in groups of four. They should show each other their work.

Plenary (10 minutes)

Talk about some of the ideas the students have had. Record items from the discussion on the whiteboard. Try to draw out the following:

- How can they know their work is accurate?
- How can they get help from the language assistant in such a way that they will learn rather than have her do all the work for them?
- Can they add a quirky, unexpected element into their work? How might they get help with that?

Homework (5 minutes)

Students should try another one of the mini-projects.

To make it harder

Find a real audience for the mini-project and help encourage the students to produce their project to the highest standard.

To make it easier

Complete one of the mini-projects with the class as a whole.

A set of mini-projects

Try one of these. Even if you don't know enough French to do these yet, work out where you would find out information to help you.

- Write a set of emails that tell a story.
- Create a fold-out brochure about your school for a visiting French-speaking student.
- Your French-speaking exchange partner is coming to stay. Using the future tense, write about the activities you have planned for him or her.
- Your family is exchanging your home with a French-speaking family so that you can have your holiday in a French-speaking country. Write a set of instructions about your home.
- You are going to work as an au pair for a French-speaking family. Write to let them know about what you can do and ask them about what your duties will be.
- You have just opened a new sandwich bar. Create a website to advertise all the wonderful new combinations customers can now purchase.
- Produce a table to show the different departments and floors in a large store. Put up the floor indicator in French.
- Find a town map or create a simple one of your own. Set up a treasure trail around it in French. This should really work. If you use your own town, you could try it out on the French exchange group.
- Create a survey that you might send to the French exchange group before they come to England to find out about what they would like to do.
- Create a survey to give to the French exchange group after they have been here to find out what they thought of the activities offered.
- Write out a shopping list for your visit to France. Write it in French so that you remember to look out for what you want to get for various friends and relations. Make a few notes about each person, so you can discuss this with the shop assistant if need be. Oh! And note the type of shop where you might find those items.
- Write some haikus about colours in French. Remember, a haiku has three lines. The first has five syllables, the second seven and the last five. Introduce a change in the last line. Write each haiku in a different colour. All the words and phrases in that haiku should be to do with your chosen colour. Write as many haikus as you can in the time allowed.

Check out *www.bonjour.com* for more ideas.

✳ **Reminders: Have you looked at your strengths and weaknesses in language learning? Have they changed? Is there anything you've used today that might help to make a difference to that balance?**

Aims and outcomes

To help students make the most of working with an exchange partner.

Materials needed

- Student Sheet 8
- interactive whiteboard
- paper for the students
- live Skype or other link to a French school

Classroom setup

Students should work in mixed-ability groups of four.

Hint

This lesson works best if your school has already set up penfriends and exchanges. It might be wise to sow the seed of that idea now if your school doesn't have such links. Try to sell the idea of Tandem Learning to your French colleagues.

This lesson works especially well if you can work via a live link to a French school or if the lesson can be performed while you are on one leg of an exchange.

Lesson starter (20 minutes)

Introduce your students to Tandem Learning. Your students are going to help the exchange students learn English, and the exchange students are going to help your students learn French.

Explain that half the activities should be in French, the other half in English; half the time the French students should be getting help, half the time the English. With two different cultures and curriculums, the needs are likely to be different. You must be careful to negotiate exactly what you need, and give your French students and colleagues exactly what they need.

Get your students to think about ideas of how the French students can help them. Examples might include going over oral topic sheets, asking the French partner to write about family homes, hobbies, pets, school, and so on, so that your students have good material to clone, and going over role plays with them. Introduce the idea of Skype, and working with the families. Students could write a not-too-personal diary and their French exchange partners could correct it for them.

Main lesson (20 minutes)

Ask the students to think of some more ideas in groups, then discuss them and write them on the whiteboard. This works even better if the English and French students work together.

Plenary (10 minutes)

Discuss the tips given on the Student Sheet for making Tandem Learning work.

Homework (10 minutes)

Students should make a Tandem Learning plan about how they can work with their partner and open up negotiations. They should try three simple ideas to start with.

To make it harder

Ask the students to produce three sets of detailed plans for three activities they might complete with their tandem partners.

To make it easier

Discuss two or three projects in detail with your students and produce a document they can use with their tandem partners.

FURTHER RESOURCES

http://tandem.ac-rouen.fr/learning/idxeng11.html gives information about Tandem Learning.

Here are a few ideas that will make work on your French with your tandem partner run smoothly.

- Remember, your French partner needs to learn English as well. Half the time you should be doing what she needs to do and half of the time what you need to do. As a consequence, you should be working half the time in French and half the time in English.

- Sometimes you should do extensive work – for example, encourage your partner to talk quite naturally and you try to follow the gist, perhaps replying in English; at other times you might insist on understanding every single word.

- You might spend some of the time correcting each other's pronunciation and grammar and other times letting a lot of that pass.

- Try to make your activities fun and highly relevant.

- Let your partner act as a model for you. She can give you some really helpful examples of language patterns and help you to learn about the part of France or any other French-speaking country she lives in.

- Be patient if your tandem partner says something you don't understand, but don't let it pass. Encourage them to make you understand, though you can also use a dictionary to help you. You must have some agreed strategies about what you will do if you don't understand. Your teacher or language assistant may be able to help with this.

- If you are doing a speaking exercise with your tandem partner on the phone, make sure you have checked who is paying for the call and that you have permission. Better still, use Skype.

- Remember all four skills – listening, speaking, reading and writing.

- You can email written work to your partner and they can check it for you, but . . .

- DON'T ASK THEM TO DO YOUR COURSE WORK FOR YOU. However, it is fine if they give you a lot of help as long as you understand everything they are doing. It will soon show if you don't and it will be obvious that you have cheated.

- You can ask your partner to help with vocabulary-building exercises – these will be introduced later in this course.

- As you work through the rest of this course, think about how you might be able to use the material with your partner.

✳ Reminders: Make yourself a list of further aspects of French you would like to learn about now.

Working with an Exchange Partner (Tandem Learning) STUDENT SHEET 8

Aims and outcomes

To prepare your students to make the most out of a trip to a French-speaking country.

Materials needed

- Student Sheet 9
- student resources to do with asking and understanding directions, shopping, ordering food and drink and coping with problems.
- town treasure trails (as above, see also extra resources below), maps and information about the place you are going to visit.

Classroom setup

There is little to do here, though you might consider conducting this in a space other than a classroom – in a small hall or a conference room, for example. You are mainly concerned with inciting enthusiasm about a trip abroad. Timings are absolutely flexible and at the teacher's discretion in this lesson.

Hint

Assume you are going on a day trip. You can adapt this lesson for a longer trip and also use some of the ideas here while on the French exchange. You need to create a 'treasure trail' around the town you are going to. Write it in French, but perhaps also provide a glossary. Use this lesson the week before you go on the trip to a French-speaking country.

Lesson starter/Main lesson/Plenary

Use as much or as little time as you need for each of the following:

1. Safety instructions. It is a good idea to have a rendezvous where there is always a member of staff or other adult on duty. When students are on their own, ask them to stay in groups of four. Two can then stay together and two can go for help if there is a problem.

2. Remind students that they are guests in the town they are visiting and are also representing their friends and family, their school and their country when there. It is of course polite to make every effort to make yourself understood and to understand the people who live there.

3. Rehearse following and asking directions, shopping, ordering food, coping with problems and general polite phrases.

4. Familiarize the students with the map of the town and any information and pictures available.

5. Familiarize the students with the town treasure trail, if you are using one.

6. Rehearse the 'writing with the senses' exercise (see Student Sheet 45)

7. Encourage students to make a note of interesting words they find. They should become language magpies.

8. Rehearse coping strategies for language problems.

Homework

Students should study the sheet provided. You may also wish to give them the town treasure trail sheet to look at beforehand, but take plenty of spares for the day.

To make it harder

Ask students to produce a questionnaire in French before you go that can be used on the day.

To make it easier

Plan a trip beforehand with all of the adult helpers. Then assign one per group who can 'scaffold' the students.

FURTHER RESOURCES

Town treasure trail sheets are available for Boulogne, Le Touquet and Berck Plage from Bridge House Languages *www. bridgehouselanguages.com*. They include a treasure trail round the town in French, a glossary, an invitation to pass tests about ordering food in cafés and shopping, a checklist of places seen, an exercise on writing with the senses and an opportunity to collect 'sign language'.

Before you go

- Revise all your phrases to do with shopping, buying food, directions and coping with problems. Ask your Tandem Learning partner to help you.
- Decide how you want to organize your work – do you want to take a plastic wallet? Do you want a special notebook for the day?
- How much money are you going to take?

Checklist for the day

- Have you got your passport?
- Have you got all the notes you need and something to write with and into?
- Have you got your camera?
- Are you taking a small dictionary?
- Is your clothing practical?

While you're there

- Carefully follow the instructions your teacher gives you. This will keep you safe.
- Try to speak as much French as you can.
- Don't panic if you don't understand. Ask people to repeat phrases slowly. Use the listening strategies your teacher has practised with you.
- Collect language. Write down any interesting words and phrases you come across while you are there. For instance, 'poubelle' means dustbin. 'Belle' means 'beautiful'!
- Remember, you can often get clues about the words and expressions you need by listening to the people around you, especially when shopping or ordering food. So, keep your ears open.
- Listen. If you can't understand all the words, you can still enjoy listening to the rhythms of the language.
- Look out for language on signs. There are words all around you. Jot some of them down or take photos. Keep your eyes open all the time.
- Look out for free reading material. Shops give it away, so does the tourist office. Gather some of it up and take it home with you.
- 'Writing with the senses' exercise. Take a few moments to stop, look, listen, smell, feel – even taste. Write down what that is like, as much as possible in French. If you are following a town trail, you will have quite a few words to remind you. You can write a few things in English as well. Enjoy all of these senses.

When you're back home

Take everything that you've collected into school and share it with your classmates, your teacher and your language assistant. Edit the work you wrote using the senses. You can now use all the resources at school to help you – and perhaps your tandem partner as well.

✳ Reminder: Try to do the above every time you go to a country where French is spoken.

Language Skills 1: Speaking

Aims and outcomes

To familiarize the students with a useful approach to role play practice.

Materials needed

- Student Sheet 10, in three separate parts, mood cards photocopied or downloaded, cut up and laminated
- other role plays you have worked on recently.

Classroom setup

Matched-ability pairs. You may therefore need to work more intensively with the less able.

Lesson starter (5 minutes)

Make sure that students understand the role play.

Main lesson (40 minutes)

Practise the role play with them.

Circulate amongst them. Don't accept that they have completed it unless they can say it backwards in their sleep without thinking about it.

Practise with the mood cards. You will need to discuss what they mean. Each student in the pair takes a 'mood' and practises the role play in that tone of voice. Then they move on to another mood.

Make sure students understand the extra vocabulary.

Allow the students to practise with the mood cards and the extra vocabulary.

Test them on the content. You could make this a team game.

Plenary (10 minutes)

Discuss with the students how they might find opportunities for practising like this. Some suggestions include:
- using the mood cards for any role play
- practising with a partner in class any time they have a few minutes spare
- practising with their tandem partner.

Homework (5 minutes)

Students learn the role play on Student Sheet 10A and practise a little more with mood cards (Student Sheet 10C).

To make it harder

Ask the students to create additional mood cards and find extra vocabulary.

To make it easier

Model each activity carefully with students as they work their way through the role plays.

Role play practice: au marché

Bonjour, monsieur, je peux vous aider?	Oh, c'est cher. Et le petit, c'est combien?
Bonjour. Je voudrais un kilo de pommes, s'il vous plaît.	*Un euro soixante-quinze.*
Voilà, monsieur. Et avec ceci?	Alors, j'en prends un petit.
Je voudrais aussi un chou.	*Voilà. C'est tout?*
Désolé, nous n'avons plus de chou.	Oui, merci.
Vous avez du choufleur, alors?	*Ça fait six euros cinquante.*
Oui. Vous désirez un grand choufleur ou un petit?	Voilà, madame.
Un grand, c'est combien?	*Merci. Au revoir, monsieur.*
Quatre euros trente.	Au revoir, madame.

================ **10: Vocabulary** ================

QUANTITÉS	FRUITS	DES LÉGUMES
Un kilo de	Cerises	Pommes de terre
Une bouteille de	Pommes	Chou
Une boîte	Oranges	Chou-fleur
Un litre de	Framboises	Petits-pois
Une livre de	Fraises	Haricots
Un paquet de	Bananes	Haricots verts
Un bocal de	Poires	Carottes
Cent grammes de	Abricots	Poireaux
	Prunes	Oignon
	Pêches	Ail
	Raisin	
	Ananas	
	Pamplemousses	

================ **10: Mood Cards** ================

Mood cards

heureux(se)	triste	déprimé(e)	ennuyé(e)	fâché(e)
impatient(e)	fatigué (e)	nerveux(se)	enthousiaste	intelligent(e)
sérieux(se)	marrant(e)	timide	courageux(euse)	poli(e)

How might you practise these with your tandem partner? When might you fit short practices in?

✳ Reminder: Can you think of other ways of working with your partner on speaking practice?

Aims and outcomes

To equip the students with general phrases that could be useful in any role play situation.

Materials needed

- Student Sheet 11
- role plays from Student Sheet 11 made into sets of cards
- Student Sheet 11 loaded on to the interactive whiteboard
- example role plays from their main textbooks (or just a set of page references)

Classroom setup

Mixed-ability groups of four.

Hint

You may find it useful to introduce your students to the 'pencil and rubber' method of learning (see Vocabulary Builder sheets, Student Sheets 48–53).

Lesson starter (10 minutes)

Get the students into groups of four. Allow the students to pair up the phrases from the Student Sheet.

Main lesson (40 minutes)

Discuss the paired phrases – use the whiteboard to give the students some examples. Leave it displayed for the next activity.

Allow the groups to play pairs. Cards are placed face down on the table and players take it in turns trying to find pairs.

Ask the groups to split into pairs. Each pair is to find a sample role play in one of the text books and see how many of the expressions they have learnt that they can get into their own role plays.

Ask each pair to perform their role play.

Plenary (5 minutes)

Quick quiz: divide the class into two teams. See which teams get the most right – first French to English, then English to French.

Homework (5 minutes)

Students are to learn the expressions from Student Sheet 11.

To make it harder

Give the students one 'useful phrase' each that they have to bring into the conversation. Once they have done that, they take another 'useful phrase'.

To make it easier

Organise a team quiz, testing the students on the 'useful phrase' – first French to English, then English to French.

FURTHER RESOURCES

www.experiencelanguage.co.uk/french/brushup/brushup.jsp for some sample role plays.

www.lefrancaisaucollege.co.uk/French_GCSE_Role_plays_English_version.doc for some sample GCSE role plays.

Je voudrais	I would like	Je dois	I must
Je peux	I can/can I?	Il faut . . .	We have to/one must
C'est possible (?)	It's possible (?)	A quelle heure . . .	At what time ...
Mais	But	Pardon monsieur /madame	Excuse me sir/madam
C'est combien?	How much is (it)?	Pour aller . . .?	How do I get to . . .
J'ai besoin de	I need	On doit . . .?	Should one/we . . .?
Je cherche	I'm looking for	Pourriez-vous . . .?	Would you be able to . . .?
Je prends	I'll have	Merci	Thank you
Bien sûr	Of course	Tu veux . . .	Do you want?
Tu aimes . . .?	Do you like?	Nous voudrions	We would like
Comment est . . .?	What is . . . like?	Il y a	There is/there are/ is there/are there
Très	Very	Trop	Too
Assez	Enough/quite	Un peu	A little
Au revoir	Goodbye	De rien	Think nothing of it
Je ne comprends rien	I don't understand anything	Où est . . .?	Where is?

✳ Reminder: Can you make up some other games with the cards? Can you learn these phrases off by heart?

Role Play 2 – General Phrases   **STUDENT SHEET 11**

Aims and outcomes

To persuade students that they don't have to learn lots of vocabulary off by heart, but that they can add and adapt from what they already know or at least have access to.

Materials needed

- copies of the students' role play sheet, Student Sheet 12
- textbooks
- students' notes
- dictionaries
- interactive whiteboard

Classroom setup

Students work in friendship groups of four.

Lesson starter (10 minutes)

Discuss Role Play 1. Make sure the students understand it and can say it well.

Main lesson (40 minutes)

Look for the easily replaceable words with the students. These are words that belong to a similar meaning group. For instance, in the first role play, these would be: arrêt d'autobus (they should know other stops – train stations, tram, metro stops, other forms of transport), école (other buildings they could go out of), centre-ville (other places they might want to go), autobus (other forms of transport), seize (other numbers), faire du lèche-vitrine (other activities they could do), hôtel de ville (other places in town), cinq minutes (other intervals of time). Make sure the students highlight them on their sheets.

Students are to think of as many words as they can for each group of words, just from Role Play 1. First, they examine each word, thinking of as many as they can for each one. Then they go though the books and their own notes. Perhaps they can take a different set each. Finally, if there is any time left, they can use the dictionaries.

Get them to find the easily changeable words in Role Play 2. Discuss the words with the students.

Let them work their way through as much of the role plays as they can.

Plenary (5 minutes)

Get the students to count up how many replaceable words they have found. Reward the winners.

Homework (5 minutes)

Students should read through the role plays carefully. They should then draw up a list of areas where they need more work, as instructed on Student Sheet 12.

To make it harder

Ask the students to find even more replacement words to fill in the role plays. They may use dictionaries, their own notes, or other text books to which they have access.

To make it easier

With the students, list on the whiteboard some useful words for using as replacements in the role plays.

FURTHER RESOURCES

www.lingolex.com/french.htm gives many lists of vocabulary.

www.speakfrench.co.uk/vocab gives vocabulary grouped in useful topics.

Role play A

Yvette Salut, Giles. Où est le prochain arrêt d'autobus?

Giles *Salut. Alors, tu sors de l'école et c'est sur ta droite.*

Yvette Merci. Quel autobus va au centre-ville?

Giles *Le bus numéro seize. Où veux-tu aller?*

Yvette Je veux tout simplement faire du lèche-vitrine.

Giles *D'accord. Dans ce cas tu peux descendre à l'hôtel de ville. Tu as un plan de la ville?*

Yvette Oui, j'en ai un. Quand est-ce qu'il y a un autobus?

Giles *Toutes les cinq minutes.*

Yvette Merci. Bonne journée.

Role play B

Jean Tu veux aller au ciné ce soir?

Anne *Oui. Qu'est-ce qu'il y a?*

Jean On montre Ma Femme est une actrice

Anne *J'ai entendu dire que c'est assez bon.*

Jean D'accord. On se donne rendez-vous où?

Anne *Devant le cinéma à sept heures et demie?*

Role play C

Alice Bonsoir. Vous avez une table pour trois personnes?

Serveur *Fumeur ou non-fumeur?*

Alice Je préfère non-fumeur.

Serveur *Par ici. Voici les cartes. Je vous laisse choisir.*

Alice Merci.

Serveur *Vous voulez un hors d'oeuvre?*

Alice Non, je préfère les desserts.

Serveur *Qu'est-ce que vous prenez comme plat principal?*

Alice Je prends le steak grillé avec pommes frites.

Now that you have worked your way through all of the role plays, which are the areas where you need to learn more? How might you improve your knowledge in those areas?

✳ **Reminder: Try to do some role play practice as often as you can.**

Role Play 3 – Adapting the Role Play   **STUDENT SHEET 12**

Aims and outcomes

To take role play out of the realms of the ordinary and into the exciting and bizarre, thus showing students that they can be as imaginative and as creative with a foreign language as they can with their own, and, most importantly, that role play does not have to be boring.

Materials needed

- Student Sheets 10, 11, 12 and 13
- other role plays (ones with which they are familiar, but photocopied again so they don't have to look for them through their books or their notes)
- textbooks
- students' notes
- the language assistant, if possible

Classroom setup

Students work in randomly formed groups of three to five.

Lesson starter (5 minutes)

Study the sample role play with the students. Make sure the students understand it and can speak it well. Make sure they understand about the hints on adapting the role plays described at the end of Student Sheet 13.

Main lesson (40 minutes)

Give each group a selection of role plays. They have two tasks: (1) to join the role plays together to form a coherent story; (2) to add in the quirky element they have found in the first role play on their sheet. This is a 'thinking outside the box' exercise. They should spend the last ten minutes rehearsing their complex, quirky role play.

Plenary (10 minutes)

Groups present their role play. You and perhaps the language assistant can comment and give marks for:
- good use of French
- how well they have used elements from other areas
- how original the story is

Homework (5 minutes)

Students are to write a screenplay titled *Dans le Chateau du Comte Dracule Partie 2*. They may consult with their tandem partner for help.

To make it harder

Groups give each other specific situations to bring into their role plays.

To make it easier

Give each group a surprise element to bring in. They should keep it secret from the rest of the class.

FURTHER RESOURCES

www.bbc.co.uk/schools/gcsebitesize/french/speakingf/f06_role_hotel_rev1.shtml gives some further examples of role plays in a hotel.

www.bbc.co.uk/schools/gcsebitesize/french/speakingh/h03_role_restaurant_rev1.shtml gives some further examples of role plays in a restaurant.

Chez le Comte Dracule

Le comte Dracule *Bonsoir monsieur, bonsoir, madame. Je peux vous aider?*

Monsieur Duval Nous voulons une chambre pour deux personnes pour deux nuits.

Le comte Dracule *Vous ne voulez pas rester jusqu'au trente et un octobre? Ça sera une soirée très intéressante.*

Madame Duval Pourquoi?

Le comte Dracule *J'ai invité des amis assez intéressants.*

Monsieur Duval Non, il nous faut partir le vingt-sept octobre.

Le comte Dracule *Dommage. Ce soir-là il y aura un grand orage terrible. Vous voulez un grand cerceuil ou deux petits cerceuils?*

Madame Duval Nous ne voulons pas de cerceuil. Nous voulons un grand lit.

Le comte Dracule *Bizarre. Comme vous voulez alors. Et vous voulez une chambre avec bain de sang ou bain de grenouille?*

Monsieur Duval Nous voulons une chambre avec douche, s'il vous plaît.

Le comte Dracule *Alors, une chambre avec douche de glace. Vous voulez dîner ce soir?*

Madame Duval Où est le restaurant?

Le comte Dracule *Le dîner, c'est à quatre heures du matin, dans la crypte.*

Monsieur Duval Et qu'est-ce qu'on sert?

Le comte Dracule *Des cœurs de grenouille, avec du sang de vampire.*

Madame Duval Ah non. Je n'en veux pas. Le petit déjeuner, c'est à quelle heure?

Le comte Dracule *A minuit, naturellement. Il y a des crapauds.*

Monsieur Duval Ah non, elle s'est évanouie.

Some hints and tips on how to make your role plays more interesting:

- Introduce less obvious items from unrelated areas. For example, bring food and drink into a role play about journeys.
- Add unusual items of vocabulary which are easy to look up, or find out from the French assistant or your tandem partner – like 'crapaud' or 'coeur de grenouille' above.
- Bring in a dramatic turn of events. A very useful area is medical problems. The waiter is late with the soup because he's just broken his leg. Or he's got an upset stomach because he tasted it.
- Have you learnt all of the general phrases for role play? Do you need to spend some more time on them?
- Can you tick off some more items from your 'big picture' – or do you now need to add on some more?

※ **Reminder: Remember to use different moods for each role play.**

Role Play 4 – Extending the Role Play　　　　**STUDENT SHEET 13**

Aims and outcomes

To shrink the task of learning all possible role plays for the students.

Materials needed

- Student Sheet 14
- copies of all the role plays you can find, including some spare sets. These can be examples from your textbooks, but also prompts and examples from old exam papers. Make sure you have covered all those listed on Student Sheet 14
- the language assistant, if possible

Classroom setup

Students work in friendship groups of four. Randomly distribute the role plays on the tables before the students come in. Assign students to tables as they enter the room.

Lesson starter (10 minutes)

Explain to students that they are going to practise then expand on as many role plays as they can in 30 minutes. They may help each other as much as they like.

Main lesson (30 minutes)

Allow the students to work through the role plays at their own pace, but ensure they do so energetically. Once they have completed the set on their desk, let them take another set.

Plenary (15 minutes)

Read through Student Sheet 14 with the whole class. Work out with them what sorts of areas of knowledge they need to have for a couple of the role play areas. For example, for shopping for food they might need to revise shops, money, quantities and asking whether something is in stock.

Homework (5 minutes)

They are to continue working through the boxes on the Student Sheet. When they have finished, they should make themselves a list of five areas they need to revise more than others – make a start on these.

To make it harder

Ask students to think of some areas not covered and do the same work for them also.

To make it easier

Limit the number of role play areas that each group covers but make sure that the class has covered all of them. You can then include feedback during the plenary.

FURTHER RESOURCES

http://sevenkingsmfl.typepad.com/gcse_french/c_role_plays provides some sample GCSE role plays.

www.quia.com/ws/334597.html helps to revise key phrases needed in role plays.

www.bbc.co.uk/schools/gcsebitesize/french/examskills/5speakingroleplayrev_print.shtml provides students with tips on how to cope with role plays.

Look at the following role play areas. Make a list in each box of all the areas of vocabulary and grammar you might need to revise to be able to perform a role play in the named area.

Shopping for food	At the sports centre
Shopping for clothes	Making arrangements to go out
Shopping for presents	Being in a French-speaking school
Finding your way around town	At the hotel
Introducing yourself to new people	Explaining about your town/home to a French-speaking friend
Talking at mealtimes	In a restaurant
Public transport	Problems with your bike/car
Health problems	At the campsite
Going to the bank	At the youth hostel

Now highlight up to five areas to which you need to give more attention. Make a start on revising them.

❋ **Reminder: It is better to do a little each day rather than trying to do too much in one go.**

Aims and outcomes

To enable students to become aware as quickly as possible of the sort of questions they might have in the oral exam. These are also useful questions for when they need to get to know someone in France.

Materials needed

- Student Sheet 15 and online version displayed
- interactive whiteboard
- dictionaries
- textbooks
- language assistance, if possible

Classroom setup

Arrange the tables so that the students can work in groups of four to six. You could let them sit in friendship groups. Put enough sheets for each student on each table.

Lesson starter (5 minutes)

Set up the task. Students are to work through the sheet, helping each other to make sure they understand what the questions mean. Start each group off at a different stage.

Main lesson (40 minutes)

Discuss what the questions mean. If there are any that the students do not understand, tease out the answer with them. You could write the answers of the more difficult questions on the board.

Now invite them to start forming their answers. Remind them that a question generally calls for information that is missing and that in this case they have to change the verb to the 'je' form from the 'tu' form. Demonstrate some examples on the board.

Let them work through the questions. If anyone becomes stuck, help them find information in a textbook. Put the page numbers on the board. You could save this for revision later.

Plenary (10 minutes)

Do a quick revision of the past and future tenses. Point out to the students the questions that make most use of each tense.

Homework (5 minutes)

Students are to finish Student Sheet 15, making their answers as full as possible. They can also use their tandem partner to check their answers and give them their own answers, which they might use as a model. If this is all finished early, students can spend more of their homework time learning the role plays.

You may want to check the students' progress at some point.

To make it harder

Ask students to form some extra questions and answers.

To make it easier

Ask students to concentrate on what they think are the five most important questions.

FURTHER RESOURCES

www.sbslangs.org.uk/frlinks.htm provides many links to help with many aspects of language learning.

Comment t'appelles-tu?

Ça s'écrit comment?

Où habites-tu?

Comment trouves-tu ta ville?

Pourquoi l'aimes-tu? Tu ne l'aimes-pas?

Il y a combien de personnes dans ta famille?

Tu as des frères ou des soeurs?

Travailles-tu ou reçois-tu de l'argent de poche?

Que fais-tu avec l'argent?

Comment viens-tu au collège?

Tu vas au quel collège?

Quelle est ta matière préférée?

Pourquoi?

Il y a une matière que tu n'aimes pas?

Quels sont vos passe-temps?

Tu aimes lire?

Que fais-tu d'habitude dans les vacances de Noël/de Pâques/pendant les grandes vacances?

Tu as déjà visité (la France) ou un autre pays étranger?

Qu'est-ce que tu y as fait?

Et le soir?

Quel temps faisait-il?

Qu'est-ce que tu as aimé le mieux?

Que feras-tu cette année pendant les grandes vacances?

Comment y voyageras-tu?

Qu'est-ce que tu vas y faire?

Où irais-tu, si tu avais beaucoup d'argent?

Tu as un correspondant français/une correspondante française?

Qu'est-ce qu'il/elle aime faire dans son temps libre?

Tu peux décrire un(e) ami(e)?

Qu'est-ce que tu aimes faire avec ton ami(e)?

Quel est ton repas préféré? Quelle est ta boisson préférée?

Tu as mangé dans un restaurant?

Comment sont les repas au collège?

Tu fais de la cuisine à la maison? Qu'est-ce que tu aimes préparer? Quelle est ta spécialité?

Il y a quelque chose que tu n'aimes pas boire/manger? Pourquoi pas?

Quel temps fait-il aujourd'hui? Quel temps fait-il d'habitude en hiver/au printemps/en été/en automne?

Qu'est-ce qu'on a dit sur la météo?

Quel temps fera-t-il aujourd'hui?

Quelle saison préfères-tu?

Pourquoi?

Hint

Get your tandem friend to help you.

❋ Reminder: Professional actors learn their lines by reading them at least twelve items. Try that with these questions.

Aims and outcomes

To prepare students to speak about themselves quite fluently.

Materials needed

- Student Sheet 16, made into cards, and also a complete sheet for each student
- examples from your textbooks and recordings of young people talking about themselves in the areas outlined on the Student Sheet
- the language assistant, if possible

Classroom setup

Arrange tables for groups of four to six people. Distribute two to three of the topics on each table. Balance harder topics with easier topics. Arrange your students into mixed-ability groups, mixing top with middle and middle with low. Have some spare cards and resources.

Lesson starter (5 minutes)

Explain the task. Students are to use the materials in front of them to enable them to speak for about two minutes on each topic. They should work through one topic at a time, formulating and then rehearsing a response.

Main lesson (40 minutes)

Circulate, perhaps with the language assistant, correcting and encouraging.

Stop the activity and hear what has been completed so far. Encourage students to work faster if they have not completed two topics. Move them on to new topics.

Students should complete two more topics in their groups.

Plenary (10 minutes)

Discuss all the prompts on the Student Sheet.

Make sure every question is understood by the whole class.

Homework (5 minutes)

Students must answer each question in writing as fully as they can. They should jot down notes on the sheet and write their answers more fully for you to check later. You may need to give them more than one homework session to complete this.

To make it harder

Ask the students to use the phrases on Student Sheet 16 to prompt each other to talk about themselves. They should attempt to answer without looking at their notes.

To make it easier

Limit students to three areas from Student Sheet 16 initially. Make sure they prepare these thoroughly before they move on to the remainder.

FURTHER RESOURCES

www.langweb.co.uk/GCSEorals/FrenchMenu.htm provides some oral practice exam papers.

Parle-moi de ta famille.	Parle-moi de ta maison.
Parle-moi de ton collège.	Parle-moi de ta ville/ton village.
Parle-moi de ce que tu aimes faire dan ton temps libre.	Parle-moi de ton ami(e).
Parle-moi de tes vacances l'année dernière.	Parle-moi de ce que tu vas faire dans les grandes vacances.
Parle-moi de ce que tu veux faire après le collège.	Parle-moi de ce que tu as fait hier soir/le week-end dernier.

These questions can also easily begin with 'Tu peux décrire . . .?'

❄ **Reminder: Are you still looking for time opportunities to fit in more language learning?**

Aims and outcomes

To extend the students' responses in oral work beyond the predictable and formulaic.

Materials needed

- Student Sheets 15, 16 and 17
- the language assistant, if possible

Classroom setup

Plan your pairs. Students are now going to work with a friend. They should have equal ability but balanced personalities and with different interests. You may need to work more intensely with less able students. These pairs may last half a term for this type of activity, but it's a good idea to change them after that point.

Hint

You may find it useful to explain that students are now engaged in an ongoing process – which will be even more enriched after Language Skills: Speaking Personal Questions 4 – Really Showing Off. Every so often, from now on, you need to take in their written versions of their oral questions and ask other questions. Then give them the language they need or correct their attempt at it. It is good to involve the language assistant with this and this is also an ideal activity to use with tandem partners.

Lower-ability students or students who are likely to be nervous on exam day might need the questions to be broken down further. Your textbooks may contain more detailed lists of questions on each topic. If not, you may need to look for another resource.

Lesson starter (10 minutes)

Conduct a mock oral with a middle-ability student, using the open-ended questions from Student Sheet 16. When she can no longer continue, ask a question from Sheet 15. Do this again with another student. Ask the others to spot what you have done.

Main lesson (35 minutes)

Let the students work through as many of these as they can in the allotted time. To save them wasting time deciding who will go first, say it should be the one who is nearest to you. They should take it in turns going over and over the sheets.

Plenary (10 minutes)

Now do another mock oral, again with a middle-ability student. Try to squeeze more information out of them on every topic. For example if they say 'Nous avons habité un hôtel' you might ask 'C'était comment l'hôtel?' Repeat this with another student. Ask them to work out what you do each time – try to use as many of the methods as possible that are mentioned on Student Sheet 17. Let them have a go.

Homework (5 minutes)

Discuss Student Sheet 17. Make sure students understand all the tips.

To make it harder

Ask the students to think of other ways of extending their answers. They could work with their tandem partner, asking him/her to extend their answers as much as possible. They should then gather interesting words and phrases they come across.

To make it easier

Work through some examples one at a time, allowing students time to note their own version and to practise them.

FURTHER RESOURCES

G. James, *French Topic Sheets* (Classroom Resources, 2001) gives further practice in a variety of role plays.

Personal Questions 3 – Extending and Enhancing Your Answers

Hints and tips on how to make your partner work harder – ask for more information

1. Added information

Ask 'Tu peux le/la/les decrire?'

For example, after she has answered:

J'habite Radcliffe.

J'ai un frère.

Je vais au college Radcliffe Riverside.

2. Ask why

'Pourquoi?' You can use this word on its own. Great if you can put it into a sentence, but your partner does not need you to.

For example, after she has answered:

Je n'aime pas les maths.

Je suis allée en ville.

Je vais travailler dans un magasin.

3. Change the tense

Que fais-tu normalement . . .?

Que feras-tu . . . (demain, le week-end prochain, pendant les grandes vacances)?

Qu'est-ce que tu as fait (hier soir, le week-end dernier, pendant les grandes vacances l'année dernière)?

4. Ask where / when / with whom

Où est-ce que tu as fait ça?

Quand/à quelle heure est-ce que tu as fait ça?

Avec qui est-ce que tu as fait ça?

And some ongoing work for you

Write out your answers to the questions on Sections 1 and 2 above. Pass them to your teacher. Ask the French assistant or your tandem partner to correct and add new questions. If you don't understand the new questions, ask for them to be translated into English. If you can't formulate your new answers, write them in English and ask your teacher, the language assistant or your tandem partner to help you.

Hint

If you have to ask for a lot of help, try to identify the areas where you need to revise and set aside some time to do this.

Reminder: Are you finding time to do a little extra French each day?

Aims and outcomes

To encourage students to get into the habit of practising the personal questions as often as possible and as effectively as possible.

Materials needed

- Student Sheets 16 and 17 on personal questions and students' own answers
- Student Sheet 18
- recording equipment
- the language assistant, if possible

Classroom setup

Pairs or individual work. See The Game, below.

Hint

If at all possible, do this exercise while the exchange group is with the students. This will enable everyone to get to know each other well.

Lesson starter (10 minutes)

Discuss Student Sheet 18. Make sure that students fully understand all the processes mentioned.

Main lesson (40 minutes)

Set up a rota for students to record their work. If possible, make this one-to-one with the language assistant. If not, let them work in pairs. If you have enough sets of recording equipment, both could take place at once. Some students can record in pairs, according to the instructions on the sheet, and others can work one-to-one with the language assistant. While the students are waiting to record or after they have recorded, they should play The Game (see below).

THE GAME

Assign each student one of the open-ended questions from Student Sheet 16. You will probably appoint several students for each one. Each student must pose the question to as many people as she can and make rough notes, in French, on their answers. They should try to get extra information from them, just as we did for Lesson 3.

Plenary (15 minutes)

Ask questions about each student. Other members of the group should contribute what they know. This will give the students some good practice in realizing that verbs have parts.

Homework (5 minutes)

Students should spend at least an hour of their own time reading and thinking about the suggestions on the Student Sheet.

To make it harder

Ask students to collate the responses they received.

To make it easier

Limit the number of open-ended questions you expect the students to answer.

Hints and tips about getting really good at these oral questions.

Work with your friend

Your teacher has put you with a friend. You should work with him/her as much as possible on these questions. Whenever there is some time at the beginning or the end of a lesson or if you finish an exercise early, run through them. Can you and your friend put aside some time each week to practise them?

If your friend is absent one day, listen in to another pair.

Your teacher will change your partner every half term.

Record questions and answers

Make a recording of the questions and answers and listen to it. You can work with your friend, or the language assistant, or your tandem partner. Listen to the recording as you walk to school, as you cook tea for your family, before you go to sleep at night. Re-record every so often – as you expand your answers as outlined below. If you work with your friend, get someone who is really good at French to listen to it and tell you if you are pronouncing the words correctly.

Expand and expand and expand

As you become more fluent at the answers you know well, use the ideas we looked at to expand your work. Never sit back. Once you can answer these questions perfectly, give them to your tandem partner, your teacher or the language assistant, who can help you expand on them. You'll then go beyond what the exam needs and soon have enough French to chat with anybody.

Work with your tandem partner. Ask him/her the questions. Get him/her to record his/her answers. Listen carefully. Is there something you can use in yours? Listen anyway – you can improve your own listening by doing that.

Use these questions in real-life situations

Generally speaking, if you're being really friendly, you don't talk about yourself all the time. It's polite to ask other people questions. Who are all those French people you heard in the park the other day? Of course you must be careful – don't do this via the internet as you never know who you're really talking to, and don't go off anywhere with those nice-looking kids in the park, but do try your French out whenever you have the chance. Even in the exam, we're delighted if you ask us a question – and it's always best in the oral exam if you do most of the talking.

If you do get the chance to use these questions in real life, listen carefully to the answers. Is there anything in them you could adapt for your own work?

Hint

Can you think of other ways of getting help from your exchange partner?

❄ Reminder: Try teaching some of your oral work to someone else – it will help you to improve.

Aims and outcomes

To enable students to make an effective presentation in French, going well beyond the requirements of the GCSE exam, or even the AS exam.

Materials needed

- Student Sheet 19
- interactive whiteboard
- the internet
- magazines – French magazines or especially produced for language students
- some good examples from former students, if you have done this exercise with other students.

Classroom setup

Students should be grouped on tables of four in mixed-ability groups.

Hint

This lesson concerns preparation for a process. The students will spend many hours on this over several weeks. Consequently, the second lesson in this series may not take place for some time. It may be helpful to set deadlines in advance (see Student Sheet 19).

Lesson starter (5 minutes)

Explain that everyone is going prepare a presentation. Talk generally about what you expect.

Main lesson (30 minutes)

Read through Student Sheet 19.

Allow the students to help each other decide on a topic.

Plenary (20 minutes)

List all the topics students are interested in doing. Group them, so that you can then talk about where they might find useful resources.

Allow students to start working through Student Sheet 19.

Homework (5 minutes)

Get students to do further work on the sheets.

To make it harder

Suggest to some able students that they pick a topic that will involve them interviewing a French speaker.

To make it easier

Show students a sample presentation from another year.

FURTHER RESOURCES

The following two companies provide magazines for French learners:

Mary Glasgow Magazines *http://maryglasgowmagazines.com*

Authentik Resources for Language Learning *www.authentik.com*

Authentik Interactive *www.authentikinteractive.com* provides online reading and listening material for French learners.

French magazines for native speakers of French can be obtained from *www.unipresse.com/?gclid=CLrDzc2i9JYCFQECGgodCmLKXQ*

The task

You are going to make a three-minute presentation to the rest of the group on a topic you love. You may use PowerPoint. The sky is the limit. After this, doing a presentation for your GCSE oral, if it is needed, will be a doddle. This activity will not only help your French, but will give you confidence about making presentations.

Timescale

The presentations to the rest of the group will take place in about six weeks' time. You will therefore need to have your text ready in about four weeks' time. Your teacher will tell you the exact dates.

Write them here: _____

Choose a topic

Get the people in your group to help you if you're stuck. They might be able to see more easily than you can yourself what would be a good topic for you. Ideas include a famous person you admire, a place you like, a hobby or an interest about which you are passionate.

Find material

Do this just as you would for preparing a presentation in English. However, look for materials in French. Use the internet, materials your teacher shows you today and others she tells you about. Your teacher, the language assistant and your tandem partner can help you with this.

Make notes and mindmaps

Gather as much material as you can and make notes and mindmaps about your findings. Do this in French. You should spend up to two-thirds of the time available in collecting material this way. Again, your teacher will suggest exact time limits for this.

Write them here: _____

Shape your presentation

Ensure you have an introduction, about three development points and a conclusion. Try to avoid lists, although if you are doing a presentation about a famous person, you might create bullet points about their CV, perhaps highlighting the most significant things that have happened to them.

Flesh out your presentation

Consider using PowerPoint or another programme to enliven your presentation. In this way you can show pictures and highlight the key points in your presentation.

Preparing the speech part

You may wish to write down the whole speech. By the time we've finished Student Sheet 20 you should be able to do the presentation from your notes. You may find some of the other lessons help you with this. You may get considerable help by going back to your raw materials. However, do not just cobble together bits of other people's text. It will make yours lumpy and it will be very clear that it is not your own.

✤ Reminder: It is important that before we go on to the Lesson 20, you have completed your script and had someone check it – either your teacher, the language assistant or your tandem partner.

Aims and outcomes

To give the students an opportunity to rehearse and enhance their presentation.

Materials needed

- Student Sheet 20
- students should bring what they need for presentation
- have computers/laptops ready
- the language assistant, if possible

Classroom setup

Again, get the students grouped around tables of four, but make sure the groups are different from last time. Provide an opportunity for students to record their work, perhaps in a separate small room, or in several places. It's a good idea to have a sign-up list and, as students return from recording, they should alert the next person on the list.

Lesson starter (5 minutes)

Tell the students what the aims of today's lesson are.

Main lesson (45 minutes)

Work through Student Sheet 20.

Get the students to work initially in pairs on the presentations. They should each do each stage before they move on to the next one. While they are doing this, circulate and correct pronunciation and intonation. Give the students tips about effective delivery.

Tell the students what you have noticed. Move them on to the second part of the sheet if they are not there already.

Plenary (10 minutes)

Allow the students to present to the other members of their table and get feedback.

How did that go? What have people noticed?

Homework (5 minutes)

Students should carry on rehearsing.

To make it harder

Ask the students to practise until they can do the presentations completely without notes.

To make it easier

Arrange an after-school session instead of homework. Invite the language assistant. Allow the students to practise and also give them as much one-to-one attention as possible.

FURTHER RESOURCES:

The following websites give you tips on looking after your voice and using it effectively:

Voice Gym *www.voicegym.co.uk*

Develop Your Voice *www.developyourvoice.co.uk/index.html*

Topic Presentations 2 – Rehearsing the Presentation

Stage 1 Reading it out loud

Practise reading your presentation out loud. Take a deep breath, right down into your belly, and speak on the out breath. Speak slowly and clearly. Look up from your work as often as you can. Remember to whom you are talking to. Repeat this exercise, taking it in turns, until you feel fairly fluent.

While you are listening to your partner, listen out for the following and give them feedback:

- Can you understand the words?
- Are they making some eye contact with you?
- Do they sound as if they understand what they are saying?
- Do they sound as if they mean what they are saying?

Stage 2 Record your presentation

As and when you are comfortable with what you are reading, and when your teacher, the language assistant or your tandem partner has checked your pronunciation, sign up for an opportunity to record your presentation. Then, while you are waiting for your turn, get on with the next section.

Speak from notes

Either highlight keywords in your text or write them out again. Help each other. Try now to speak just from those.

While your partner is speaking, place their text in front of you and prompt them as required.

Which works better? Reading from notes or reading out the whole speech from a script?

Stage 3 Integrate visuals

Once you can speak quite well from your notes, practise integrating your visual aids, for instance, a PowerPoint slide show.

Prompt your partner as needed and stop them if they are mistiming slides or other visuals.

Once you have your timing right, or when your teacher tells you, show your presentations to the other people at your table.

Give feedback on all aspects: the content, use of language, use of visuals, interest.

- What is good?
- What is not so good?
- What might they do to improve?

Stage 4 Further practice

Carry on with all of the above. Listen to your recording. Practise with your partner. Practise with someone who has not heard it yet – Mum, Dad, grandparents, brothers and sisters, even the cat or the dog!

❄ Reminder: Try to build time for practice into every day.

Topic Presentations 2 – Rehearsing the Presentation   **STUDENT SHEET 20**

Aims and outcomes

To encourage a natural reaction in French in the audience and in the presenters' response to that reaction.

Materials needed

- Student Sheet 21
- interactive whiteboard
- computers/laptops
- the language assistant, if possible
- students should bring their presentations and any material they need to support them

Classroom setup

Set up tables so that students can work in groups of six to eight. Form your groups so that students are working with people they have not worked with before on presentations.

Hint

It is a good idea to save your and your students' suggestions on your interactive whiteboard. These ideas will be helpful when it comes to revision.

Lesson starter (10 minutes)

Read Student Sheet 21.

Main lesson (20 minutes)

Allow the students to work through Student Sheet 21. Go around from group to group, correcting pronunciation and offering ideas.

Plenary (20 minutes)

Discuss some of the things you have noticed.

Students should then carry on working through the Student Sheet.

Hold a second plenary. What have they noticed?

Homework (10 minutes)

Emphasize the last part of the Student Sheet, which tells them how to carry on working on this which they should attempt for homework.

To make it harder

Ask the students to give their feedback in French.

To make it easier

Watch several presentations with the whole class, drawing out comments from your students.

FURTHER RESOURCES

The following websites give tips about using the interactive whiteboard:

Interactive whiteboards in learning and teaching *http://dis.shef.ac.uk/eirg/projects/wboards.htm*

Interactive whiteboards *www.inquiringmind.co.nz/interactive_whiteboards.htm*

You are now going to help the people in your group make their presentation even better.

When you are listening

Jot down any questions you want to ask. Ask for help with formatting the questions if you find this difficult. Your teacher or the language assistant may be able to help during the lesson. If there are still some questions you need to complete after the lesson has ended you can ask your tandem partner.

You can include some of the types of questions you used in your general conversation work from Student Sheets 15, 16 and 17:

- added information – 'Tu peux le/la/les décrire?'
- ask why – 'Pourquoi?' – you can use this word on its own; your partner does not need you to put it into a sentence but you can try if you want to.
- ask when something has happened or will happen.
- ask where/when something takes place.

Write down what the language assistant or teacher suggests and try to learn it.

After you have listened

Give the presenter general feedback about content, language, the way they spoke and the way they used visuals.

- What did you like?
- What was less impressive?
- What could they do to improve?

When you are presenting

Remember to breathe deeply and speak on the out breath.

Make sure you remember who you are speaking to and stop worrying about yourself.

If you don't understand the questions, ask the teacher or the language assistant to help. Write down what they say and try to learn it.

Don't take any negative comments as criticism of you. They are action points you need to take to help you improve.

Ongoing work

Continue to work on your presentation. Get as many people as you can to ask questions and practise the answers.

✳ **Reminder: Are you also remembering to practise your personal questions?**

Aims and outcomes

To allow students to enjoy the work they have completed on presentations and to leave the lesson with some thoughts about what they might improve even further.

Materials needed

- Student Sheet 22 for individuals or groups – see below – this depends to some extent on how you decide to run the lesson, which in turn depends to some extent on the size of your group
- visual aid support needed by the presenters

Classroom setup

For large and medium groups, organize groups of tables facing the presenter's area. Arrange the students into groups of four to six 'judges', preferably in combinations that they have not used in other presentation lessons. Smaller classes could work as a whole.

Hint

This lesson can be conducted in various ways. If you have a very large group, you may have to spread the lesson over several lessons – perhaps the last half of the lesson. If you have a small group you may consider letting students vote individually. For medium-sized groups you may wish to complete it all in one lesson. Alternatively, you may prefer to do three per lesson until they are completed. Or you could turn it into an occasion and have an afternoon off – does your timetable allow for this? Do you want to award prizes?

Lesson starter (5 minutes)

Make sure students understand how to fill in their voting sheets.

Mark one presentation with the group. It is wise to pick a student who will be good and to arrange this beforehand.

Main lesson (40 minutes)

Allow the presentations to take place. The voting forms should be filled in after each presentation.

Plenary (10 minutes)

Find out results. Who has been voted the best? More importantly, make sure that everybody gets their feedback sheets. Encourage all the students to take this in good spirit, celebrating their good points and taking note of their weaker points. They should examine their peers' suggestions and decide whether these are useful action points.

Homework (5 minutes)

To carry on working on the presentations. You may also find by now that your students have acquired quite a few language learning skills and habits and know their own strengths and weaknesses. If they are already confident about their presentations, they may be able to self-direct themselves to other tasks for homework.

To make it harder

Invite an outside audience in – perhaps involving some native speakers of French.

To make it easier

Allow students to present to smaller groups. You could organize a round robin, where half of the class present to a group at a time. They move from table to table to do this. Instead of using a classroom data projector, they could use individual laptops.

Voting sheet

Name of presenter: _____

Title of presentation: _____

Tick which statement for each area you most agree with. This determines the score.

Content

This was really interesting, perhaps even funny in places and had lots of information.	5	
This was quite good and the presenter told us many interesting facts.	4	
This was fair and the presenter kept going for the whole time.	3	
This had a few interesting facts, but was a bit short and dull.	2	
This was very short and we didn't learn much.	1	

French

The presenter talked fluently, with a good accent, good intonation and we could understand her well.	5	
The presenter spoke quite fluently, with quite a good accent and quite good intonation and we could understand her quite well.	4	
The presenter was a little hesitant, though their accent and intonation were reasonable and we could understand her if we listened carefully.	3	
The presenter was hesitant and their accent and intonation did not sound much like French. They were quite hard to understand.	2	
The presenter was very hesitant. Their accent and intonation was very poor. We could hardly understand them.	1	

Presentation skills

The presenter was really confident. They had very good eye contact with the audience. Their timing and use of visuals was great.	5	
The presenter was quite confident. They had good eye contact with the audience. Their timing and use of visuals was quite good.	4	
The presenter was confident some of the time. They had some eye contact with the audience. Their timing and use of visuals was good some of the time.	3	
The presenter was not very confident. They had little eye contact with the audience. Their timing and use of visuals was sometimes poor.	2	
The presenter had little confidence. They hardly looked at the audience. Their timing was not very good at all and they hardly used any visuals.	1	
	Total	

What is the biggest change they could make to improve their presentation?

✳ **Reminder: Always start and end with the positive when giving feedback.**

Language Skills 2: Listening

Aims and outcomes

To make students more aware of the situations in which we need to listen and how we listen.

Materials needed

- Student Sheet 23
- audio files – available from the Continuum Companion website, *http://education.james.continuumbooks.com*
- interactive whiteboard

Classroom setup

Students should work individually in this lesson. You may need to book a computer room so that the students can access the audio files. It is also very useful to be able to play the audio files through a central speaker. Use the interactive whiteboard for writing down student responses.

Lesson starter (15 minutes)

Get students to listen to the audio files and jot down what they think is happening in each one.

Students should listen to the files three times, filling in the Student Sheet as they go along.

Main lesson

(30 minutes)

Discuss the answers with the students. Available at *http://education.james.continuumbooks.com*

Subjects are:

1. You are in a supermarket and they are making announcements about products that are on offer.
2. You are at a station and they are telling you which trains are arriving and departing, which platform and whether or not they are on time.
3. You are in a school that has a public address system and the head teacher is giving the news of the day.
4. You are at a bus stop and you are listening to two people planning what they are going to do that evening.
5. Someone has left you a message on the phone. They are telling you that a book that you have ordered has arrived.
6. You are listening to a weather forecast.

Discuss with the students how they worked out what was going on. Note the answers on the whiteboard. Use two columns. What did they recognize because they recognized the French? What did they recognize because of something else? Point out how we can often assess the meaning of the French by the clues we get from other non-linguistic sounds and we should learn to be 'sound' detectives.

Explain that we are now going to take this a stage further and listen individually to the files. Discuss Student Sheet 23 and make sure they understand it.

(20 minutes)

Students should listen to the files a further two times, filling in the Student Sheet as they go along.

Plenary (10 minutes)

Discuss what they have found. Discuss the whole experience of listening. Did listening for certain items help, or was it easier to just listen generally?

Homework (5 minutes)

This is outlined on Student Sheet 23.

To make it harder

Ask the students to make notes on any interesting or useful phrases they hear.

To make it easier

Complete some of the sections on Student Sheet 23 with the students as they listen. Pause the audio file after each unit of sound.

Listening three times to an audio file in French is always recommended. The first time you get a general impression. The second time, you begin to get more details. The third time you will probably understand everything except the words you have never met and to which there is no clue. The only way you'll understand those is by learning more French. You might be surprised at how much more you understand after the third time you listen in comparison to the first time. It's a bit like finding the pieces of a jigsaw puzzle and suddenly seeing the picture emerge.

You have already listened to these six situations with your teacher. You might, however, like to listen once more for a general impression.

Second Listening

Write down all the places you hear:

1.

2.

3.

4.

5.

6.

Third Listening

Now, listen again, and write down as much detail as you can about what has happened in each situation. Use the back of this sheet.

Homework

Try these listening exercises:

Better Listening *www.bbc.co.uk/languages/french/listening*

French Extra *www.francais-extra.co.uk/gateway/listening/listeningindex.htm*

FSL All Listening *www.fslall.com/learn_french_297.html*

❋ **Reminder: Learning vocabulary can also help you with your listening.**

Listening Situations   **STUDENT SHEET 23**

Aims and outcomes

To give students more insight into how they can improve their listening.

Materials needed

- Student Sheet 24
- use any 5 minute audio file where the students are likely to understand most of the vocabulary because of what they have already learnt
- computers
- interactive whiteboard

Classroom setup

Students work individually.

Lesson starter (10 minutes)

Discuss areas of vocabulary that might come up in listening situations. These are similar to the vocabulary areas encountered in role play situations. Let the students work in pairs to think of more.

Main lesson

(15 minutes)

Discuss the students' lists and summarize them on the whiteboard. Look at the checklist on Student Sheet 24. Have any areas been missed out?

(10 minutes)

Recap what you learnt about listening in Lesson 23. Discuss how we get clues from things other than French and how we get clues from areas of vocabulary within the text of the file. Remind them about listening three times.

(15 minutes)

Let students listen to the audio file at least three times and work through the Student Sheet at their own pace.

Plenary (5 minutes)

Discuss answers. Discuss how they got on with the listening exercise and working through the questions.

Homework (5 minutes)

Set one of the following listening tasks for homework.

To make it harder

Ask the students to make a note of any useful vocabulary or phrases they hear.

To make it easier

Limit the number of areas of vocabulary you ask the student to research on Student Sheet 24. You could divide the tasks out between the students.

FURTHER RESOURCES

These are some places where you can find more audio files:

Free Language *http://freelanguage.org/learn-french/skill-enhancement/improve-french-listening-skills*

French Foundation Listening

www.teachnet-uk.org.uk/2006%20Projects/MFL-Foundation_Listening/1FoundationListening/Index.htm

Decoding What You Hear

The listening task

Listen to the recording once, then answer this question:

What would you say the recording was basically about?

Listen to it a second time. As you do, answer the following questions in your workbook:

Which words do you recognize?

What quantities do you hear?

What times do you hear?

Which places do you hear?

Write down any words you think may be important but which you didn't understand.

Listen a third time

Write down at least ten details about what happened. If you have time left, listen again and try to fill in more detail for all questions.

Listening situations

Think about areas of vocabulary you need to learn for the following situations. Make a mindmap and a revision guide for each one. You can jot down on this sheet ideas you think of in class.

Shops

Restaurants

Staying with an exchange partner

French school

Travelling

Public transport

Making friends

Dealing with problems

Holidays – campsites, youth hostels, hotels

Directions

Getting about town

Talking about the future

Work

Hobbies

Families

Reminder: Can you speak about the topics above?

Aims and outcomes

To familiarize the students with the type of questions they will face on listening tasks and to equip them with tools for tackling them.

Materials needed

- Student Sheet 25
- interactive whiteboard
- examples of questions from listening papers
- one medium-difficulty listening exercise (15 minutes maximum)

Classroom setup

Arrange groups of four around tables. Put a selection of the listening exercises on each table. Take care to see that there are a good selection of the different types on each table. This time, the students should work in ability groups.

Hint

It is often useful to use exam papers from another board than the one you are using, although you may need to compensate for a different style. You may stumble across something as yet unused by your board but planned for this year.

Lesson starter (10 minutes)

Put the headings from Student Sheet 25 on the board. Discuss the headings, making sure the students understand what each type of exercise means. Ask them to find an example of each sort from the pile on the desk.

Main lesson

(15 minutes)

Ask the students to work through the headings and make notes, looking at what needs to be done to answer each type of question. Ask each group to start at a different question, giving the lower-ability students the simpler one and the higher-ability the harder ones.

(10 minutes)

Keep notes on the whiteboard, and save them for the revision file. Ask students to make notes on their sheets as you go through. Point out that part of the homework is to spend some time familiarizing themselves with these different approaches to the listening questions and revising any areas they are weak in. Give out Student Sheet 25.

(15 minutes)

Complete the listening exercise. Remind students about listening generally first, then for detail, and then for working out what is likely to happen in the situation they have identified.

Plenary (10 minutes)

Discuss answers to the listening exercise.

Homework (5 minutes)

Students should try listening to another audio file at home.

To make it harder

Restrict the audio files to the level of GCSE Higher Listening and harder.

To make it easier

Listen to one of the exercises as a whole class. As you find the answers with students, discuss the ideas on Student Sheet 25.

FURTHER RESOURCES

Aqa old papers *www.aqa.org.uk/qual/gcse/french_a_assess.php* (free)

NGFL past papers *www.wjec.co.uk/index.php?subject=57&level=7&imageField2.x=39&imageField2.y=8* (free to registered users)

Below are some hints and tips on how to tackle the questions in listening tasks. Add your own notes.

Simple questions in English

Make sure you give all details. Look at the number of points. Guess after the third listening – it isn't actually guessing, it's just using another part of your mind. Don't leave any blanks.

Matching a picture and what you hear (Ecrivez la bonne lettre)

Work out what you might hear if each picture is the one needed but beware of red herrings. Don't leave any blanks.

Completing detail in French

Look at the number of marks. Use the words given in the questions as hooks for things to listen out for. Think of what the answers might be or which types of word fit grammatically in the gap.

Choosing from a list

Work out what the list means. Listen out for those items.

Filling in boxes

Work out what the box means. Practise making notes in French. Match the number of marks given to the number of details you give.

Gap-filling in French

Work out what the French you have in front of you means. Anticipate what sort of things might go in the gap.

More complex questions in English

Work out what French you are likely to hear. Match the amount of detail you give to the points awarded for the answers. NEVER LEAVE ANY GAPS.

How did you get on with the listening exercise today? Did you remember to listen first for the general situation and then for specific details?

Did the way you listened pinpoint an area you need to revise?

❋ Reminder: Are you still learning a little new vocabulary each day?

Aims and outcomes

To enhance students' listening skills and to show them how to use listening to enhance their other skills.

Materials needed

- audio file – available from the Continuum Companion website, *http://education.james.continuumbooks.com*
- Student Sheet 26
- put a copy of the audio transcript on the whiteboard, to be revealed later; or make a photocopy for each student.

Classroom setup

Students work individually.

Lesson starter (5 minutes)

Remind students of what they have learnt about listening.

Main lesson (45 minutes)

Follow the Student Sheet.

Transcript (available at *http://education.james.continuumbooks.com*):

Marc Salut, Jeanne. Tu vas au ciné ce soir avec la clique? On va manger après. On va prendre une pizza, peut-être.

Jeanne *Je ne sais pas, moi. Qu'est-ce qu'vous allez voir?*

Marc Je ne sais pas. Un film comique, je crois. C'est plutôt pour être avec les copains. On s'amuse bien avec tout le groupe.

Jeanne *Bon, aller au cinéma et puis manger, je ne sais pas. Je fais des économies.*

Marc Mais au Grand Rex, il y a une réduction pour les étudiants. Puis on va manger dans la pizzeria Saint Michel. Tu peux partager une pizza avec moi.

Jeanne *D'accord, alors. On se rencontre où?*

Marc Chez toi? On peut prendre le bus ensemble.

Jeanne *Et à quelle heure?*

Marc A six heures et demie. Il y a un bus à sept heures moins vingt. On arrivera en ville à sept heures cinq. On a dit que le film commence à sept heures vingt.

Jeanne *Et on rentre à quelle heure?*

Marc Après le film et la pizza? A vingt-deux heures?

Jeanne *Non. Ça ne va pas! Le dernier autobus part à vingt et une heures et demie.*

Marc Alors on peut prendre un taxi.

Jeanne *Mais non, j'ai déjà dit. Je fais des économies.*

Marc C'est ennuyant. Tu es ennuyeuse. Pourquoi fais-tu des économies?

Jeanne *Parce que je veux m'acheter une moto. J'en ai marre des autobus qui ne roulent pas le soir. C'est presque impossible de sortir le soir.*

Marc Tu ne viens pas alors, ce soir?

Jeanne *Malheureusement, non. Je reste chez moi et j'étudie. On se voit demain en classe.*

Answers (1) go to the cinema/with the gang/go and eat afterwards/have a pizza [4 marks], (2) what the film is [1 mark], (3) be sociable [1 mark], (4) she's saving [1 mark], (5) student reductions/she can share his pizza [2 marks], (6) 19.05 [1 mark], (7) last bus is at 9.30 [1 mark], (8) taxi is only choice/she is trying to save for motorbike [2 marks], (9) she's fed up of not being able to go out in the evening [1 mark], (10) stay at home/and study [2 marks]

Plenary (5 minutes)

Check how the class has got on with this work.

Homework (5 minutes)

Ask the students to do what they can to enhance their listening skills. They might try one of the further resources.

To make it harder

Ask the students to make notes in French as they listen to the audio file for the first time.

To make it easier

After the students have listened to the file once, discuss in English what they have heard.

FURTHER RESOURCES

The following websites give further practice in listening comprehension:

About French *http://french.about.com/library/listening/bl-listeningindex.htm*

Ciel France *www.ciel.fr/learn-french/comprehension-exercises.htm* (Try B1)

Multilingual Books *www.multilingualbooks.com/freelessons-french.html*

The listening exercise

Remember to listen to the audio file three times. The first time, just listen for the gist.

Listen again and answer as many of the questions below as you can. Notice the number of marks awarded and try to give the right amount of detail.

Listen for a third time. Then fill in all the answers – guessing if you are not sure.

1. Give four details about what Marc suggests for the evening. [4 marks]
2. What does Jeanne ask about? [1 mark]
3. What, according to Marc, is the main point of the trip? [1 mark]
4. Why does Jeanne hesitate? [1 mark]
5. How does Marc persuade her to go out? [2 marks]
6. What time will they arrive in town? [1 mark]
7. What is the problem with coming back by bus? [1 mark]
8. Why does Jeanne decide not to go in the end? [2 marks]
9. Why does she want to do this? [1 mark]
10. What does she now plan to do this evening? [2 marks]

Now try this

Listen again. Can you write out the conversation? Spend no more than 15 minutes on this.

Check your work

Ask your teacher for the answers and the transcript of the audio file. Check your answers. If there is anything you don't understand, ask your teacher.

Some more things to learn

Is there anything else you need to learn? Are there any broad areas of vocabulary that you need to revise?

If there is time

Use the transcript of the tape for role play practice. Do you realize you have now practised all four skills – listening, reading, speaking and writing – this lesson? We often learn through listening BUT sometimes it is hard to recognize what we already know when we hear it.

✷ **Reminder: Spend some time collecting and learning vocabulary.**

Aims and outcomes

To enhance students' listening skills and to show them how to use listening to enhance their other language skills.

Materials needed

- Student Sheet 27
- audio file – available from the Continuum Companion website *http://education.james.continuumbooks.com*
- put a copy of the transcript on the whiteboard to be revealed later, or make a photocopy for each student

Classroom setup

Students work individually.

Lesson starter (5 minutes)

Make sure that students understand the Student Sheet.

Main lesson (40 minutes)

Students work though Student Sheet 27

Transcript (available from the Continuum Companion website *http://education.james.continuumbooks.com*):

(Noise of restaurant)

La serveuse Je peux vous aider?

Jean *Alors, je voudrais manger. Je peux voir la carte?*

La serveuse Bien sûr, monsieur. Voilà. Et nous avons aussi les trois menus à prix fixe. Il y a le menu à quinze euros, à vingt euros et à vingt-trois euros. Vous les voyez au tableau noir.

Jean *Je ne sais pas. Il faut que je reflechisse …*

La serveuse Alors, je vous laisse. Vous voulez une boisson?

Jean *Oui, une eau minérale, s'il vous plaît.*

(Noise of restaurant)

La serveuse Voilà. Une eau minérale. Vous avez choisi?

Jean *Je prends le menu à vingt euros. Pour commencer, les crudités et puis le poulet rôti.*

La serveuse Vous voulez des frites ou de la salade?

Jean *Des frites.*

La serveuse Et vous voulez du pain?

Jean *Oui, bien sûr.*

(Noise of restaurant)

La serveuse Vous avez fini?

Jean *Oui, merci, il y en avait un peu trop.*

La serveuse Mais c'était bien?

Jean *Oui, oui, c'était délicieux.*

La serveuse Vous voulez voir la carte des desserts?

Jean *Il me faut être à la gare à deux heures vingt. Je voudrais l'addition s'il vous plaît.*

Answers (1) A, (2) C, (3) C, (4) A, (5) A, (6) A, (7) C, (8) B

Plenary (10 minutes)

Discuss students' progress through Student Sheet 27.

Homework (5 minutes)

Ask students to continue with the extra exercises from Student Sheet 27.

To make it harder

Ask the students to make notes of what they have heard in French.

To make it easier

After students have listened to the audio file once, discuss its content with them in English.

The listening exercise

Remember to listen to the audio file three times. The first time, just listen for the gist.

Now read the questions and answers below carefully: work out in your head as many possible answers as you can think of for each question.

Listen again and answer as many of the questions as you can.

Listen for a third time. Then choose your answers, guessing if you are not sure. DO NOT LEAVE ANY GAPS.

Ecrivez la bonne lettre.

1. Jean demande à la serveuse:

   A. a menu   B. blackboard with €15 menu   C. blackboard with €20 menu

2. Quel est le bon tableau?

   A. blackboard with menus at €20, €23 and €25.   B. blackboard with menus at €15, €20 and €25.   C. blackboard with menus at €15, €20 and €23.

3. Qu'est-ce que Jean prend comme boisson?

   A. a Coke   B. a coffee   C. a mineral water

4. Il prend le menu à:

   A. €20   B. €15   C. €23

5. Pour commencer il prend:

   A. raw vegetables   B. soup   C. pâté

6. Comme plat principale il prend:

   A. chicken and chips   B. salad and chips   C. chicken and salad

7. Il ne mange pas tout parce que:

   A. he doesn't like the food   B. it is ten past two   C. there is too much food

8. Il ne prend pas de dessert parce que:

   A. he feels sick   B. he doesn't have time   C. the dessert is too expensive.

Other things to do until the end of the lesson and for homework

Write out the conversation. Ask your teacher for the answers and the transcript of the audio file. Check your answers.

Is there anything you need to learn? Are there any broad areas of vocabulary that you need to revise?

Use the transcript of the tape for role play practice.

✳ Reminder: Can you fit in some more role play practice?

Aims and outcomes

To enhance students' listening skills and to show them how to use listening to enhance their other language skills.

Materials needed

- Student Sheet 28
- audio file – available from the Continuum Companion website *http://education.james.continuumbooks.com*
- put a copy of the transcript, available from the Continuum Companion website *http://education.james.continuumbooks. com*, on the whiteboard to be revealed later, or make a photocopy for each student

Classroom setup

Students work individually.

Lesson starter (10 minutes)

Give out Student Sheet 28 and make sure students understand what they need to do.

Main lesson (40 minutes)

Students work though Student Sheet 28.

Transcript (available from the Continuum Companion website *http://education.james.continuumbooks.com*):

(Noise of busy department store)

Le vendeur Bonjour mademoiselle, je peux vous aider?

Nicole *Je cherche un cadeau pour mon petit frère. J'aime bien ces T-shirt, mais je ne connais pas sa taille.*

Le vendeur Il a quel âge, votre frère?

Nicole *Il a sept ans, mais il est plus grand que les autres garçons dans sa classe.*

Le vendeur Je crois que ce T-shirt serait la bonne taille.

Nicole *Oh, vous ne l'avez pas en bleu?*

Le vendeur Je regrette, nous l'avons seulement en rouge. Mais nous avons aussi les pulls – en bleu et en rouge.

Nicole *Ils sont a combien, les pulls?*

Le vendeur Ils coûtent €54.

Nicole *Non, ils sont trop chers.*

Le vendeur Nous avons aussi ces casquettes-ci. Il y une offre – vous pouvez en a avoir deux pour le prix d'une. Et nous les avons en bleu et en rouge. Elles sont à vingt euros.

Nicole *Super! J'en prends une en bleu pour mon petit frère. Et j'en prends une en rouge pour ma sœur.*

Le vendeur Alors, voilà, mademoiselle. Ça fait €20. Vous voulez autre chose?

Nicole *Et vous pouvez me dire où se trouve le café? Je vais m'acheter une glace maintenant que j'ai acheté tous mes cadeaux.*

Answers (1) son frère, (2) sa taille, (3) grand, (4) sept, (5) rouge, (6) rouge/bleu [2 marks], (7) 54, (8) chers, (9) une offre, (10) des casquettes, (11) 20, (12) sa sœur, (13) au café, (14) une glace

Plenary (5 minutes)

Check how students have progressed through the Student Sheet.

Homework (5 minutes)

Ask the students to continue working through the Student Sheet.

To make it harder

Make up another conversation like this in a different sort of shop.

To make it easier

When you show the students the transcript of the audio file, check with them that they understand all of the words.

The listening exercise

Remember to listen to the audio file three times. The first time, just listen for the gist.

Now read all the phrases below carefully. Work out in your head what you might hear in each gap.

Listen again and fill in as many of the gaps as you can.

Listen for a third time. Then fill in all the answers, guessing if you are not sure. DO NOT LEAVE ANY GAPS.

1. Nicole achète un T-shirt pour _____.

2. Elle ne sait pas _____.

3. Son frère est assez _____.

4. Il a _____ ans.

5. Le vendeur a le T-shirt seulement en _____.

6. Il a les pulls en _____ et _____. [2 marks]

7. Ils coûtent _____ euros.

8. Pour Nicole, ils sont trop _____.

9. Il y a _____ – en acheter une, en emporter deux.

10. Il a aussi _____ en bleu et en rouge.

11. Elles coûtent _____ euros.

12. Nicole en achète une rouge pour _____.

13. Elle veut aller _____.

14. Elle va s'acheter _____.

Other things to do until the end of the lesson and for homework

Write out the conversation. Ask your teacher for the answers and the transcript of the audio file. Check your answers.

Is there anything you need to learn? Are there any broad areas of vocabulary that you need to revise?

Use the transcript of the tape for role play practice.

✳ **Reminder: Learn some of the words that frequently crop up in role plays.**

Aims and outcomes

To enhance students' listening skills and to show them how to use listening to enhance their other skills.

Materials needed

- Student Sheet 29
- audio file available from the Continuum Companion website *http://education.james.continuumbooks.com*
- put a copy of the transcript, available from the Continuum Companion website *http://education.james.continuumbooks. com*, on the whiteboard to be revealed later, or make a photocopy for each student

Classroom setup

Students work individually.

Lesson starter (5 minutes)

Make sure students understand Student Sheet 29.

Main lesson (40 minutes)

Students work through Student Sheet 29.

Transcript (available from the Continuum Companion website *http://education.james.continuumbooks.com*):

Alain Bon, les salles de classes 34 à 45 sont dans ce bâtiment. Ce sont plûtot les classes de cinquième et du quatrième. Nous avons nos cours dans le bâtiment D.

Michelle *Le collège est assez grand, alors. Il y a combien d'élèves en tout?*

Alain Il y en a mille deux cents. Et puis, il y a le lycée à côté. Encore deux cents étudiants.

Michelle *C'est pratique, ça, d'avoir le lycée tout proche, comme ça.*

Alain Je ne sais pas. Il y a toujours des problèmes avec les bus. Mais ça va pour les internes.

Michelle *Il y a des internes?*

Alain Oui, il y a une trentaine d'étudiants qui arrivent le lundi et passent les nuits de lundi à jeudi dans le lycée.

Michelle *Je détesterais ça.*

Alain Je ne sais pas. Avec tous les problèmes avec les transports … Le trajet me prend deux heures chaque jour.

Michelle *Bon. Je vais venir en moto.*

Alain Alors, il te faudrait une autorisation du directeur.

Michelle *C'est difficile d'obtenir ça?*

Alain Je ne sais pas. Il faut demander au bureau.

Michelle *Et comment sont les profs?*

Alain Pas mal, en général. Ils sont assez sympas. Sauf Madame Renoir. Elle est comme une sorcière. Elle est très désagréable et assez stricte.

Michelle *Elle est prof de quoi?*

Alain Anglais.

Michelle *Oh non. Je suis très faible en anglais.*

Alain Pas de problème aujourd'hui. Elle est malade. Bon, allons à la cantine.

Answers (1) faux, (2) vrai, (3) vrai, (4) faux, (5) pas mentioné, (6) vrai, (7) pas mentioné, (8) vrai, (9) pas mentioné, (10) pas mentioné, (11) vrai, (12) vrai, (13) faux, (14) pas mentioné, (15) vrai, (16) pas mentiné, (17) vrai.

Plenary (10 minutes)

Check how students have progressed through Student Sheet 29.

Homework (5 minutes)

Students should be asked to continue with the exercises from Student Sheet 29.

To make it harder

Ask the students to make a second role play based on the transcript of the audio file.

To make it easier

Ask the students just to make notes about what they hear. Reveal the transcript at a point in the lesson when most students have listened to the audio file enough. Make sure they understand all the words and phrases.

The listening exercise

Remember to listen to the audio file three times. The first time, just listen for the gist.

Now read all the sentences carefully. Work out what you might hear if they are true.

Listen again and fill in as many of the gaps as you can.

Listen for a third time. Then fill in all the answers, guessing if you are not sure. DO NOT LEAVE ANY GAPS.

	Vrai	Faux	Pas mentioné
1. Il y a trente-cinq salles de classe dans ce bâtiment.			
2. Ce sont pour les classes du cinquième et du quatrième.			
3. Michelle aura ses cours dans le bâtiment C.			
4. Il y a trois milles cent élèves en tout.			
5. Tous les élèves iront plus tard au lycée.			
6. Il y a une trentaine d'internes.			
7. Ils viennent de la campagne.			
8. Alain voyage deux heures chaque jour.			
9. Michelle a besoin d'un permis de conduire.			
10. Alain n'a pas de moto.			
11. Les profs sont sympas.			
12. Madame Renoir est très stricte.			
13. Elle est prof de français.			
14. Michelle est assez forte en français.			
15. Madame Renoir est malade aujourd'hui.			
16. Alain a faim.			
17. Ils vont à la cantine.			

Other things to do until the end of the lesson and for homework

Write out the conversation. Ask your teacher for the answers and the transcript of the audio file. Check your answers.

Is there anything you need to learn? Are there any broad areas of vocabulary that you need to revise?

Use the transcript of the tape for role play practice.

✳ **Reminder: Revise all your vocabulary and spoken and written answers to questions about school.**

Listening Exercise 4 **STUDENT SHEET 29**

Aims and outcomes

To enhance students' listening skills and to show them how to use listening to enhance their other skills.

Materials needed

- Student Sheet 30
- audio file available from the Continuum Companion website *http://education.james.continuumbooks.com*
- put a copy of the transcript on the whiteboard to be revealed later, or make a photocopy for each student

Classroom setup

Students work individually.

Lesson starter (5 minutes)

Make sure that students understand Student Sheet 30.

Main lesson (40 minutes)

Students work through Student Sheet 30.

Transcript (available from the Continuum Companion website *http://education.james.continuumbooks.com*):

Germaine Qu'est-ce que tu vas faire cet été?

Robert *Je pars en vacances avec Charles et Yvon. On va faire du camping dans les Pyrénées.*

Germaine Tu aimes les montagnes, alors. Je préfère aller à la plage.

Robert *Tu pars aussi en vacances?*

Germaine Malheureusement, non. Je dois garder ma sœur cadette. Ma grand-mère est malade et mes parents prennent tout leur congé annuel pour lui rendre visite, pour vendre sa maison pour lui trouver une maison de retraite.

Robert *Dommage. Elle a quel âge, ta sœur?*

Germaine Elle a dix ans.

Robert *Ça va être ennuyant pour toi. Qu'est-ce que tu vas faire alors?*

Germaine Ce n'est pas trop mal. On ira à la piscine. Elle est invitée chez des amies plusieurs fois. La météo est bonne. On peut se faire bronzer dans le jardin.

Robert *Mais quand même. Tes parents, ils vont rester chez ta grand-mère combien de temps?*

Germaine Quatre semaines.

Robert *C'est beaucoup. Mais, tu ne peux pas partir après?*

Germaine Non. Quand mes parents rentrent, a la fin de juillet, je vais faire un stage chez le journal France Aujourd'hui.

Robert *Excellent. Ça doit être très intéressant. De toute façon, beaucoup plus intéressant que mon boulot au café, Chez Pierre.*

Germaine Tu fais toujours ça?

Robert *J'ai besoin de l'argent. Mais ça va s'arrêter en septembre quand je retourne au lycée. Mon père m'a dit qu'il me donnera plus d'argent de poche afin que je puisse me concentrer plus sur mes études.*

Germaine Tu as de la chance. C'est bien avec le journal, mais après, il me faut continuer dans le magasin.

Answers

(1) go camping/with friends/in the Pyrenees [3 marks], (2) go to the beach [1 mark], (3) she has to look after her sister [1 mark], (4) take holiday/visit her grandmother, sell her house, look for old people's home [4 marks], (5) 10 [1 mark], (6) they can go to the swimming pool, her sister has lots of invitations, the weather is going to be good, she can sunbathe [4 marks], (7) end/July [2 marks], (8) work for a newspaper [1 mark], (9) in a café [1 mark] (10) it is boring [1 mark], (11) father will give him extra pocket money/so he can concentrate on studying [2 marks], (12) she still has to work in the shop [1 mark]

Plenary (10 minutes)

Check the students' progress through Student Sheet 30.

Homework (5 minutes)

Students should continue with the work from Student Sheet 30.

To make it harder

Ask the students to make up another role play based on the transcript of the audio file.

To make it easier

Ask the students just to make notes about what they hear. Reveal the transcript at a point in the lesson when most students have listened to the audio file enough. Make sure they understand all the words and phrases.

The listening exercise

Remember to listen to the audio file three times. The first time, just listen for the gist.

Now read all the sentences carefully. Work out what you might hear in order to be able to answer the question.

Listen again and answer as many of the questions as you can.

Listen for a third time. Then fill in all the answers, guessing if you are not sure. DO NOT LEAVE ANY GAPS.

1. What is Robert going to do for his holidays? [3 marks]

2. What does Germaine prefer to do? [1 mark]

3. Why has she got to stay at home this time? [1 mark]

4. What are her parents doing? [4 marks]

5. How old is Germaine's sister? [1 mark]

6. Why doesn't Germaine think it will be too bad? [4 marks]

7. When will her parents be back? [2 marks]

8. What is she going to do then? [1 mark]

9. Where does Robert work? [1 mark]

10. What does he think of his job? [1 mark]

11. Why will he be able to give up his job in September? [2 marks]

12. Why does Germaine think Robert is luckier than her? [1 mark]

Other things to do until the end of the lesson and for homework

Write out the conversation. Ask your teacher for the answers and the transcript of the audio file. Check your answers.

Is there anything you need to learn? Are there any broad areas of vocabulary that you need to revise?

Use the transcript of the audio file for role play practice.

Revise all your work about holidays and schools.

Make up another discussion about people's future plans.

Talk with your exchange partner in French about your plans for the summer and for after you leave school.

✳ **Reminder: Revise your prepositions.**

Listening Exercise 5   **STUDENT SHEET 30**

Aims and outcomes

To enable students to become proactive in their listening, to work in ways that will give them more practice at listening and to use listening as a tool for learning.

Materials needed

- Student Sheet 31
- interactive whiteboard
- internet access, if possible
- all the textbooks and reference materials the students are used to working with
- a collection of audio files/CDs and the means to play them separately
- the language assistant, if possible.

Classroom setup

Equal-ability groups with four to six to a table. You may have to work more with the less able groups.

Hint

Often when you buy audio CDs as part of a course, you buy the right to make copies for every student at the institution. Others are accessible over the internet via your site license. Why not set up a catalogue and a lending facility so that your students can work their way though your files topic by topic and/or order of difficulty?

Lesson starter (5 minutes)

Explain the aim of the lesson.

Main lesson

(10 minutes)

Students to work through the lists on Student Sheet 31. They should find resources that help them with vocabulary. They should be listed on the sheet.

(10 minutes)

Show your students the audio resources and how they can access these themselves.

(10 minutes)

Discuss how recently they have used the listening exercises to help them with producing scripts for speaking. Listen to an audio file with them now and discuss which words and phrases might be useful to them in producing spoken language.

(10 minutes)

Individually, students should make plans of what they are going to listen to in the next two weeks, and then how they will fit listening practice into their busy lives after the two weeks.

Plenary (10 minutes)

Go to the website *http://radiotime.com/genre/c_143/French.aspx*. Discuss with the students some of the programmes they might like to listen to. Listen to a few seconds of some of their suggestions. Discuss which ones might be useful.

Homework (5 minutes)

Students should spend some more time using the above website. Alternatively, if you do have a bank of listening resources, they could start working through these.

To make it harder

Students can be asked to add three categories to the ones listed on Student Sheet 31.

To make it easier

You could limit each student to three categories from Student Sheet 31. They can later share ideas with their peers.

Listening is a passive skill – you need a passive knowledge of vocabulary to understand what is being said. You need to know what French words mean in English. Listening, however, can be an active activity in that it can also help you to learn French.

We recently looked at the areas listed below. Can you think of any more? Where can you find help in your resources? Write page numbers and books next to each one.

Shops

Restaurants

Staying with an exchange partner

French school

Travelling

Public transport

Making friends

Dealing with problems

Holidays – campsites, youth hostels, hotels

Directions

Making friends

Getting about town

Talking about the future

Work

Hobbies

Families

Use listening to help you learn more French words and expressions and to improve your fluency.

What did your teacher suggest? Have you thought of any other ideas?

What will you do over the next two weeks to enhance your listening?	After that, how will you make listening a habit?

Remember French Radio *http://radiotime.com/genre/c_143/French.aspx*

❈ **Reminder: Remember to do some reading for pleasure.**

Language Skills 3: Reading

Aims and outcomes

To introduce the student to intensive reading, to make them understand the difference between this and extensive reading and to familiarize them with habits that will help them with intensive reading.

Materials needed

- Student Sheet 32
- dictionaries
- other photocopied reading materials (these should be photocopies rather than originals so that students can write on the sheets)
- interactive whiteboard

Classroom setup

Students should work in pairs. Approximate-ability pairing should work well for this.

Lesson starter (5 minutes)

Explain the difference between intensive and extensive reading: in intensive reading the student aims to read a short text and understand every word; in extensive reading they aim to understand the gist of a larger text. Intensive reading can also improve students accuracy, while extensive reading can improve their fluency and also increases their passive knowledge.

Main Lesson

(5 minutes)

Distribute Student Sheet 32. Read the text out loud.

(5 minutes)

Make sure they understand the instructions. Let them pick out the words they know.

(5 minutes)

Go to the second stage. Let them highlight the words that resemble English.

(5 minutes)

Go to the third stage. Let them do 'detective' work on what is still obscure.

(5 minutes)

Read and interpret the whole text with them. Point out that if this isn't part of an exam, they might use a dictionary. If it is part of an exam or other assessment, they would now have to make sensible guesses.

Also encourage them to make notes of words they did not know and learn them passively.

(15 minutes)

Let the students work through several other texts in the same way.

Plenary (10 minutes)

Check some of the students' work.

Homework (5 minutes)

Give each student another reading task for homework.

To make it harder

Provide the students with an extra piece of intensive reading material – such as a short article from a magazine written for people their age.

To make it easier

Have the main intensive reading exercise from Student Sheet 32 on the whiteboard. As you discuss the suggestions on the Student Sheet, mark up the text on the board.

An Introduction to Intensive Reading

Intensive reading means very careful reading. You study a text until you really understand every single word. Usually, however, any work you do after three readings does not help all that much. You may then need to consult an expert – your teacher, the language assistant, or your tandem partner.

How to approach intensive reading

1. Read the text for the first time. Make notes on what you understand.

2. Read the text for a second time. You'll probably understand a lot more this time. If you can, read it aloud. If you're in a situation where you can't read aloud, imagine your voice or someone else's reading it. You may notice that some of the words sound surprisingly like English.

3. Read it for a third time. You will understand a lot more this time. Some words will only have one possible meaning now. Many will have a limited range of meanings.

The text

Notre maison est assez grande. Il y a trois étages. Nous avons quatre chambres au premier étage et un grand salon au deuxième étage. Dans ce salon, nous pouvons regarder la télévision le soir, ou jouer à l'ordinateur. Il y a une petite cuisine là-haut et une salle de bains. Il y a une autre salle de bains au premier étage. Au rez-de-chaussée il y a un autre salon – C'est plutôt pour nos parents. Ils y reçoivent les invités. Il y a aussi une cuisine et un petit cabinet de travail. J'y fais mes devoirs. C'est plus tranquil. Mes deux frères jouent leur musique trop haut dans leurs chambres.

J'aime ma chambre quand même. Quand mes frères ne sont pas à la maison, C'est assez agréable. Ils sortent souvent. Charles a dix-neuf ans et Marc a vingt-trois ans. Ils travailllent pendant la journée et le soir ils jouent au football ou ils vont au bistrot prendre un verre avec des copains. Mais après le travail et avant de sortir ils font beaucoup de bruit dans leurs chambres. Exactement quand je veux faire mes devoirs.

Dans ma chambre il y a mon lit, mon armoire, ma table, mon étagère avec tous mes livres, et mon ordinateur. J'ai même une télévision. Mais je préfère regarder la télé dans le grenier. Le poste y est plus grand.

Nous habitons cette maison depuis deux ans. Avant nous habitions dans la ville. Il y avait beaucoup de bruit à cause de la circulation. Ici, C'est plus calme et plus prorpe. J'aime beaucoup habiter à la campagne. Il y a le seul problème que C'est difficile de sortir le soir. Mais j'ai de la chance. Tous mes deux frères savent conduire. Il me conduisent chez des copains en ville, ou au centre-ville pour aller au ciné, ou pour rencontrer mes copains dans un café.

Au village près de notre maison, il y a un club de jeunesse absolument super. J'y ai beaucoup d'amis. On fait beaucoup de choses. Et ici à la campagne on peut faire des promenades.

Oui. J'adore habiter ici. Notre jardin est très joli aussi – surtout en été.

It is a good idea to make a note of all the words you have not seen before.

✳ Reminder: Practise a basic role play.

Aims and outcomes

To enable students to use their intensive reading skills to interpret and answer questions and to form their own models for writing.

Materials needed

- Student Sheet 32 and 33
- dictionaries
- other reading texts (one of which you might like to keep for homework)

Classroom setup

Same pairs as for previous lesson.

Hint

Although most exam boards are phasing out the questions in the target language to be answered in the target language at GCSE, being able to answer such questions is still an appropriate language skill, particularly if students wish to continue their studies. It is excellent practice for intensive reading and also helps with writing.

Lesson starter (5 minutes)

Explain the link between questions and intensive reading. Point out that a question is actually a sentence with a missing piece of information.

Main lesson

(10 minutes)

Allow the students to read and interpret the text, using the intensive reading principles they learnt in Lesson 31.

(10 minutes)

Explain what the questions mean. Point out the question words. Explain to the students that they don't need to give full sentence answers at this stage.

(10 minutes)

Let them work out the answers.

(10 minutes)

Check the answers with them. Then model how questions can become answers – take out the question word, reorder the sentence if need be, and supply the missing information. Explain the use of pronouns instead of nouns where appropriate e.g. (1) Comment est la maison de Nicole? 'Comment' = what like, alter word order, put in an adjective, and replace 'maison' with 'elle' = Elle est grande. (2) Combien d'étages y a-t-il dans sa maison? 'Combien' = 'How many?' Change the word order and say how many. Replace 'étages' with 'en' = Il y en a trois.

Answers (also available on the Continuum Companion website). Note: answers here are full sentences. They don't need to be in the exam. Here we are also practising forming sentences by getting help from the questions. Also, these are just suggestions.

(1) elle est grande, (2) il y en a trios, (3) il y a quatre chambres, (4) il est au deuxième étage, (5) on y peut regarder la télé ou jouer à l'ordinatuer, (6) il y en a deux, (7) il est au rez-de chaussée, (8) ses parents l'utilisent, (9) elle y fait ses devoirs, (10) c'est plus tranquil, (11) oui, elle l'aime, (12) il a dix-neuf ans, (13) ils travaillent, (14) ils jouent au football ou ils vont au bistrot prende un verre, (15) ils font du bruit avant de sortir, (16) Nicole veut faire ses devoirs, (17) il y a son lit, son armoire, soen étagère, ses livres, son ordinateur et une television, (18) elle préfère regarder la télévision dans le grenier, (19) elle y habite depuis deux ans, (20) c'est calme et propre, (21) il y avait beaucoup de bruit à cause de la circulation, (22) c'est difficile de sortir le soir, (23) il la conduisent chez les copains, (24) il est absolument super (25) on peut faire des promenades.

Plenary (10 minutes)

Explain that they should try the rest of the questions, giving answers in full sentences. Try a few more with them.

Homework (5 minutes)

Students should finish off the questions for homework.

To make it harder

Ask the students to find some more examples of questions as part of their homework.

To make it easier

As you check the questions with the students, elicit answers from them and provide them with other examples.

The questions

Study the questions below using what you learnt about intensive reading.

1. **Comment** est la maison de Nicole?
2. **Combien d'**étages y a-t-il dans sa maison?
3. **Qu'est-ce qu'il y a** au premier étage?
4. **Où** est le grand salon?
5. **Qu'est-ce qu'**on y peut faire?
6. **Combien de** salles de bains y a-t-il?
7. **Où** est l'autre salon?
8. **Qui** utilise ce salon?
9. **Qu'est-ce que** Nicole fait dans le cabinet de travail?
10. **Pourquoi?**
11. **Est-ce que** Nicole aime sa chambre?
12. **Quel** âge a Charles?
13. **Que** font les deux frères pendant la journée?
14. **Et** le soir?
15. **Quand** est-ce qu'ils font beaucoup de bruit?
16. **Pourquoi** est-ce que ça est mal?
17. **Qu'est-ce qu'il y a** dans la chambre de Nicole?
18. **Où est-ce qu'elle** préfère regarder la télé?
19. **Depuis quand** habite Nicole dans cette maison?
20. **Quels** sont les avantage d'habiter ici?
21. **Quels** étaient les désavantages d'habiter dans la ville?
22. **Quel** est le seul problème?
23. **Comment** est-ce que les frères aident Nicole?
24. **Comment** est le club de jeunesse?
25. **Qu'est-ce qu'**on peut faire à la campagne?

Notice the question words in **bold**. Make a note of them and what they mean. Learn them off by heart as soon as you can.

Notice how some of the question words alter the word order.

Some question words are followed by 'est-ce que'. Why do you think this is?

✻ **Reminder: Consider why grammar is important. Make sure you understand the main points – verbs, word order, prepositions, parts of speech, numbers, and gender.**

Aims and outcomes

To give students more practice in intensive reading and to show them how they can use this skill to help with their writing.

Materials needed

- Student Sheet 34
- dictionaries

Classroom setup

Get the students to work in equal-ability pairs – perhaps different from the ones they worked in for the previous two sheets.

Lesson starter (5 minutes)

Remind students about how to tackle intensive reading.

Main lesson

(10 minutes)

Students work through the text on the Student Sheet.

(5 minutes)

Check that the students have understood the passage.

(10 minutes)

Students read through the questions and answer them simply.

(5 minutes)

Check that students have understood what the questions mean and discuss the answers.

(10 minutes)

Show them how to 'clone'. This is taken up also in the 'writing' lessons. Students should substitute the words in bold with another similar word. Do a few examples with them.

Students carry on 'cloning' this text on their own.

Plenary (10 minutes)

Check some of the 'cloned' answers with the students. Make sure they understand the principle. Remind them of how to make fuller answers.

Homework (5 minutes)

Complete 'cloning' and answer questions in full.

Answers (available from the Continuum Companion website *http://education.james.continuumbooks.com*).

(1) dans la boulangerie/de son oncle [2 marks], (2) du pain/des gâteaux/du chocolat [3 marks], (3) le petit déjeuner/du café [2 marks], (4) samedi/jeudi [2 marks], (5) 6 ½ [1 mark], (6) 14.00 [1 mark], (7) 17.30 [1 mark], (8) les clients/les autres qui y travaillent [2 marks], (9) nettoyer les vitrines [1 mark], (10) €12/heure [2 mark], (11) €20 [1 mark], (12) sa mère [1 mark], (13) il sort/avec des copains [2 marks], (14) dimanche après-midi, (15) va au centre de sports/jouer au basket [2 marks]

To make it harder

Ask them to list at least three words they can use for all of those marked in bold on the student sheet.

To make it easier

Provide the students with a selection of words they might use for the 'cloning' exercise. Make sure this list includes several appropriate ones.

FURTHER RESOURCES

Bonjour de France *www.bonjourdefrance.com/index/indexapp.htm* provides some extra reading practice.

Intensive Reading and Building Sentences

Remember the rules for intensive reading. If you've forgotten, look back to the previous lessons.

The text

J'ai un petit boulot. Je travaille **dans la boulangerie de mon oncle**. Enfin, c'est plutôt une boulangerie-pâtisserie – ou même une boulangerie-pâtisserie-confiserie. On y vend **du pain, des gâteaux et du chocolat.** Il y a même un petit café où on peut prendre **le petit déjeuner ou un café.**

J'y travaille le **samedi** et le **jeudi après-midi. Le samedi** je commence à **huit heures et demie** et je finis à **trois heures. Le jeudi après-midi** je commence à **quatorze heures** et je finis **à dix-sept heures trente**.

J'aime bien **les clients et les autres gens qui y travaillent**, mais je n'aime pas **nettoyer les vitrines.**

Je gagne **douze euros par heure.** Je reçois aussi **vingt euros** comme argent de poche **par semaine** de **ma mère.** Je fais des économies pour **aller en vacances.**

Le **samedi soir je sors avec des copains.** Parfois **je vais au match de foot le dimanche après-midi.** Ou je vais **au centre de sports** pour **jouer au basket**.

1. Où est-ce que Jean travaille? [2 marks]
2. Qu'est-ce qu'on y vend? [3 marks]
3. Qu'est ce qu'on peut prendre au café? [2 marks]
4. Quels jours est-ce que Jean y travaille? [2 marks]
5. Il travaille combien d'heures le samedi? [1 mark]
6. A quelle heure est-ce qu'il commence le jeudi? [1 mark]
7. Et à quelle heure est-ce qu'il finit? [1 mark]
8. Qu'est-ce qu'il aime? [2 marks]
9. Qu'est-ce qu'il n'aime pas? [1 mark]
10. Combien est-ce qu'il gagne? [1 mark]
11. Combien d'argent de poche est-ce qu'il reçoit? [1 mark]
12. Qui lui donne ça? [1 mark]
13. Qu'est-ce qu'il fait le samedi soir? [2 marks]
14. Quand est-ce qu'il va parfois au match de foot? [1 mark]
15. Qu'est-ce qu'il fait s'il n'y a pas de match? [2 marks]

Now try to write out full answers to the questions

Remember to write down any new words, including any question words you have not met before and learn them. Have a go at producing your own text – replace the words in **bold** with words that function in the same way to produce an alternative text.

Reminder: Revise your verbs, perhaps looking particularly at 'voice'.

Aims and outcomes

To give students more practice at intensive reading and to show them how to form their own questions.

Materials needed

- Student Sheet 35
- dictionaries
- other reading exercises
- samples of reading in textbooks
- interactive whiteboard

Classroom setup

Get the students into groups of four by putting the pairs from the previous lesson together.

Lesson starter (5 minutes)

Remind the students of the rules for intensive reading.

Main lesson

(15 minutes)

Let students interpret the reading passage on the Student Sheet.

(5 minutes)

Check with them what they think the text means.

(5 minutes)

Revise question words.

(20 minutes)

Show them how to build questions. This is in effect the reverse of what they did before when they turned questions into statements. They are taking information out of a sentence and replacing it with a question word or expression.

Each group creates ten questions and then passes them on to another group who answers them. When they have created all the questions they can think of for this text, they can try doing some questions on another text.

Plenary (5 minutes)

Ask each group to give you one of their questions for you to write on the whiteboard.

Homework (5 minutes)

Students can create a set of questions for another reading text – perhaps one they have in their textbooks.

To make it harder

Ask each group to pass their questions to another group to review.

To make it easier

During the plenary, make up questions with the students and write them on the whiteboard. They will refer to the work they did earlier, but any mistakes will be corrected as you put the questions on the board. This way, you can supply the students with a 'clean' set of questions.

FURTHER RESOURCES

The following resources give help with asking questions in French:

About French *http://french.about.com/library/weekly/aa022600t.htm*

How to ask questions in French *www.french-linguistics.co.uk/grammar/questions.shtml* and *http://wordpress.com/tag/how-to-ask-questions-in-french*

Learn French *www.learnfrenchlanguageguide.com/learn-french-grammar/asking-yes-no-questions-in-french*

Question words *www.thisfrenchlife.com/thisfrenchlife/2005/12/asking_question.html*

A French beginner *http://france-say.blogspot.com/2008/08/how-to-ask-questions-in-french.html*

Remember how to approach intensive reading:

1. Read the text for the first time. Make notes on what you understand.

2. Read the text for a second time. You'll probably understand a lot more this time. If you can, read it aloud. If you're in a situation where you can't read aloud, imagine your voice or someone else's reading it. You may notice that some of the words sound surprisingly like English.

3. Read it for a third time. You will understand a lot more now. Some words will only have one possible meaning. Many will have a limited range of meanings.

The text

Ma meilleure amie s'appelle Claudine. Elle a seize ans. Elle est grande et mince. Elle a de longs cheveux blonds. Elle a les yeux bleus. Elle habite Paris. Elle habite un beau apartement au cinquième étage dans un grand immeuble près du centre de la ville. Elle y habite avec ses deux frères et sa petite soeur. Son père travaille dans une banque et sa mère est professeur ici au collège.

Je connais Claudine depuis quatorze ans. Nous jouions ensemble dans le parc pendant les vacances quand nous étions plus petites. Nous allions à la même école primaire et à la même école maternelle aussi. Nous sommes comme des soeurs jumelles.

Nous avons aussi les mêmes passe-temps, sauf qu'elle sait aussi faire de l'équitation. Elle a de la chance. Son oncle est fermier, et elle lui rend visite à la ferme chaque année. Elle y reste une quinzaine, pendant que je m'ennuie à la maison. J'aimerais aussi faire du cheval.

Cepedant, nous faisons beaucoup ensemble. On est même parti en vacances de neige l'année dernière. Nous savons très bien faire du ski. On a vite appris ça. Nous savons aussi patiner, jouer au basket et tricoter. J'ai tricoté un beau pull bleu pour mon père.

Au collège, c'est la même chose. Nous sommes toutes les deux fortes en anglais et français et nulles en maths et sciences naturelles.

Mon anniversaire, c'est le quinze mai et son anniversaire est le dix-huit mai.

Mais maintenant tout change un peu. Claudine est malade. Il lui faut passer quelques semaines à l'hôpital. C'est assez grave. Elle va perdre tous ses beaux cheveux à cause de tous les médicaments qu'il lui faut prendre.

Il faut que je sois assez courageuse pour elle.

Remember how to make questions

Make a list of your question words. Look at the Student Sheets on intensive reading we have already done. Look through your textbooks.

Remember the different forms:

    Question words and 'est-ce que'.

    Question words and reverse word order.

    No question word and just change your voice at the end of the sentence.

Now make up as many questions as you can about this text and one other.

✳ Reminder: Try to read a little French each day.

Aims and outcomes

To instil the habit of effective intensive reading in students.

Materials needed

- Student Sheet 36
- shorter, simpler texts suitable for intensive reading
- some materials that are useful for extensive reading
- dictionaries

Classroom setup

Whole class and individual.

Hint

Can you build up a bank of intensive reading activities, of varying difficulty and subject? There are several schemes available on the market.

Lesson starter (15 minutes)

Discuss the following points:

- Reading can be a passive skill, and is easier the more vocabulary a learner knows. Discuss ways of building vocabulary, especially if you have not yet done the vocabulary-building exercises.
- Remind students of the meaning of intensive reading (understanding every word).
- Discuss the best ways to approach this task (three readings, decoding as you go along, then turn to the dictionary, the expert or sensible guess work).
- Discuss what else they can gain from intensive reading (help with writing and vocabulary-building).

Main lesson (20 minutes)

Allow the students to work through the Student Sheet. Try to find the opportunity to speak to each student about their game plan for improving their intensive reading.

Plenary (10 minutes)

Discuss some of the ideas that students have had so far.

Homework (15 minutes)

Students should work on their plan for the remainder of the lesson and complete this for homework.

To make it harder

Ask students to keep a reading diary. They should list what they read, how this has helped them and what they might do next.

To make it easier

Extend the plenary by 5 minutes to allow time for creating a generic action plan for the whole group.

FURTHER RESOURCES

The following resources provide extra intensive reading practice:

Jaqui et Jaqueline *www.zigzageducation.co.uk/synopses/2420.asp?filename=2420*

Classroom Resources French Reading Scheme *www.classroom-resources.co.uk/acatalog/Online_Catalogue_MFL_French_Reading_Scheme_1337.html*

Carte Blanche Revilo *www.revilolang.com/schools_cards.cfm*

Intensive reading – a passive skill

With Intensive reading you need to recognize what French means. In order to do well in this skill, you need to build up your vocabulary. Write some notes about how you will do this, and any areas of vocabulary that you think you particularly need to revise.

What do you need to know?

How will you go about that?

How long can you spend each week on this?

Intensive reading means understanding every word

Not only that – how is the grammar working? But don't worry if you haven't done the grammar lessons yet.

Intensive reading strategies

Remember; three goes is the optimum. After that use sensible guesses, an expert or a dictionary.

How good are you at this? Do you need more practice?

Make some notes on how you might fit in more practise of this skill.

Hint

Ask your teacher whether she has a bank of reading materials you could work through. When you start on this, pick the right level, but also be prepared to stretch yourself.

Most of the time, choose the areas where you know you need to improve; but if you're getting through these well, allow yourself about 10 per cent of the time to choose those areas that you find most interesting.

What else might you gain from practising intensive reading?

Writing practice and vocabulary building.

Make notes about how you will integrate this into your work over the next few weeks.

Now write yourself a 'to do' list

Focus on what you might do over the next two weeks to improve your intensive reading. Also think of how you might include some of the activities mentioned in the section above.

Hint

The very last line in your list should be your plan for reviewing your intensive reading.

Show your teacher your list. Once it has been approved, start working on it. Homework is, of course, more of the same.

❄ Reminder: Build up your vocabulary by writing acrostic poems.

Aims and outcomes

To introduce students to extensive reading and the strategies for making it easier.

Materials needed

- Student Sheet 37
- some extensive reading materials – this can include onscreen items

Classroom setup

Students are most likely to benefit from this is if they work individually, but allow talking and sharing of work – this can be quite helpful for this type of activity.

Hint

It is a good idea to supply a bank of extensive reading materials. Encourage students to help themselves.

Lesson starter (10 minutes)

Discuss extensive reading. Explain to the students that this is using reading for all the same things that they do in their own language except that it won't be quite the same experience. They will not understand as much as they do in English nor as much as they do when reading intensively. They may well, however, understand all they need to know.

Reading through three times can still be helpful, but they may not have time in a real-life situation.

Main Lesson

(10 minutes)

Show them some extensive reading materials.

(20 minutes)

Let the students pick a couple of extensive reading samples. They should read for 20 minutes and make notes about what they have read.

Plenary (10 minutes)

Discuss what they have read. Go around the whole class if time permits.

Homework (10 minutes)

Allow students to select two more pieces of extensive reading to take home. Explain that they will be expected to report back next lesson (which may or may not be the next extensive reading lesson).

To make it harder

Ask the students to keep or add to a reading diary (see Teacher Sheet 36). If they are doing this or are about to start doing this, they are probably ready to take three pieces of reading rather than two for homework.

To make it easier

As the students complete their individual reading, help less able students work out which material is easy for them and which will stretch them. Suggest ways to help them improve.

FURTHER RESOURCES

Some useful websites for onscreen reading:

Yahoo in French *http://fr.yahoo.com/index_narrow.html*

Google in French *www.google.ca/intl/fr*

Amazon in French *www.amazon.fr*

The news in French *http://news.google.fr*

French television *http://videos.tf1.fr/video/news* and *www.france2.fr*

What is extensive reading?

This time you are not trying to understand every word, though it is still useful to read the passage three times. If you cannot understand it at all after three goes, it is probably too hard for you. Try something labelled 'easier'. You are, however, only expected to understand the gist and some things are easy to understand even when there are a lot of words you don't recognize. Try not to look up more that one word per page, though looking up words is a good way of learning new vocabulary.

If you don't have to look up any words, the piece of reading is probably too easy for you.

Some types of extensive reading

Below are some types of text that might help with extensive reading. The most difficult is at the top:

- books written for French-speaking people your age
- magazines written for French-speaking people your age
- brochures and pamphlets without many pictures
- brochures and pamphlets with lots of pictures
- websites
- books and magazines written for French-speaking people who can't read very well.
- books and magazines written for people learning French.

Pick something to read

Try something from the list – your teacher will tell you where the resources are. If it's too hard or too easy use the list above to find something else.

Hint

When you are sure of which level suits you best you could ask your tandem partner to send you some more examples.

Reporting back

Make some notes of what you have read today. Report back to the rest of the class.

Homework

Have a look at two more extensive reading texts and report back to the rest of the class next time. Try to write down one new word you come across from each page.

Hint

Try to fit in some extensive reading in French on a weekly or daily basis. Can you make it such a habit that you don't actually notice you're doing it?

What about surfing the internet in French?

Can you make a list of some of the operating language? Try *www.yahoo.fr* for instance.

✳ Reminder: Work with your tandem partner to build up your vocabulary.

Aims and outcomes

To encourage students to consider extensive reading in French as part of normal life.

Materials needed

- Student Sheet 38
- access to the internet, with safeguards, but enabling searching in French
- notebooks

Classroom setup

Ideally, students should be working individually, but if you do not have enough computers you might allow them to work in twos or threes.

Lesson starter (5 minutes)

Make sure students understand the Student Sheet. If possible, guide them through the first search.

Main lesson

(20 minutes)

Allow them to complete the exercises on their sheets.

(5 minutes)

Discuss answers with them.

(5 minutes)

Explain how to set up a new search. Students should make a list of new items for their peers to look for on the internet. This needs to be completed in Word, copying the style of the Student Sheet, and be printed off before the end of the lesson.

(10 minutes)

Students complete their questionnaire for other students to answer.

Plenary (10 minutes)

Organize printing and distribution.

Homework (5 minutes)

The students complete each other's internet search lists for homework.

To make it harder

Ask students to invent a search for their tandem partner. They should ask their tandem partner to invent a search for them in turn – perhaps with the prompts written in French.

To make it easier

Extend the plenary to give enough time for you and the class to invent another search together. Students can then complete this for homework.

FURTHER RESOURCES

The Language Teachers Guide to the internet

www.classroom-resources.co.uk/acatalog/Online_Catalogue_The_Language_Teacher_s_Guide_to_the_Internet_1352.html and Internet for Language Learning *www.vts.intute.ac.uk/he/tutorial/langs* provide the teacher with tips on how to use the internet to aid language teaching and learning.

The following are useful French search engines:

Yahoo *www.yahoo.fr*

Google *www.google.fr*

Amazon *www.amazon.fr*

You are going to use the internet to practise extensive reading. Note the most useful new word you learn on each screen in your workbook. It may well be an operating term.

1. Use *www.amazon.fr* for the following:

   a to find a present for your French-speaking penfriend, exchange partner or tandem partner

   b to find the name of a novel written by Alexandre Dumas

   c to find out about a bestselling book in France at the moment

2. Use *www.yahoo.fr* to find out the following:

   a the weather in Paris today

   b your horoscope for today

   c a TV programme in French you would like to watch – note which channel and what time it is on

3. Use *www.google.fr* to find out the following:

   a where the tourist office in Toulouse is

   b what is on at the cinema in Lille

   c a campsite you would like to visit in the Pyrenees

4. Use the most appropriate search engine you can think of to find out ten facts about a town that you've heard of. Make a note of what you have found out. Remember to record one new word for each screen you look at.

5. Pick a sport that you like. Find out five things about what is happening in that sport next weekend.

6. Find out about a school in France. Write down ten facts about it in English.

7. Find out where you can get some bargains in France. Look for the following items:

   Jeans

   Ski equipment

   Cheap hotels

   CDs by your favourite bands

   A cheap flight from Paris to London Heathrow

8. Look for some recipes, involving the following ingredients:

   Eggs

   Potatoes

   Tomatoes

REMEMBER TO DO ALL YOUR SEARCHES IN FRENCH. You should have written down at least 43 new words. Finished? Now create a similar treasure hunt for a friend.

✳ **Reminder: Revise your French word order.**

Aims and outcomes

To instil in students the idea that reading for pleasure is possible in another language (even though it may not be quite the same experience as reading in their own language) and that it can become a habit that will aid them in their acquisition of French.

Materials needed

- Student Sheet 39
- lots of examples of extensive reading materials
- books and magazines written for French-speaking people of their age, brochures and pamphlets without many pictures, brochures and pamphlets with lots of pictures, websites, books and magazines written for French-speaking people who can't read very well and books and magazines written for people learning French
- internet access
- dictionaries

Classroom setup

Make the classroom as conducive to relaxed reading as possible. Students will probably work individually. If possible, provide some refreshments, or allow the students to bring some in to share. Try to programme such informal lessons every now and then – or leave such lessons for a cover teacher. This lesson is ideal for the end of the day.

Hint

It may now seem like a good idea to keep a bank of materials that students can access at all times and does not need to be heavily supervised.

Lesson starter (5 minutes)

Explain the lesson. Make sure they understand the Student Sheet.

Main lesson (40 minutes)

Just allow the students to read.

Plenary (10 minutes)

Discuss the experience with them.

Homework (5 minutes)

Ask them to make a plan to do some more reading for homework.

To make it harder

Push the students to read at the level above which they feel comfortable.

To make it easier

Allow the students to read at the level at which they feel comfortable. Help them to define this by working one-to-one with the students as they read.

FURTHER RESOURCES

Mary Glasgow Magazines *http://maryglasgowmagazines.com*

Authentik *www.authentik.com/magazines.html* provide magazines that are easy for learners to read.

French books which are easy to read can be found at:

http://shop.linguascope.com/acatalog/Readers_French.html

Online magazines in French are available from:

http://w3.coh.arizona.edu/french/uoa/magazine.html

Relaxed reading

Today we are going to concentrate on reading for pleasure. You might consider at the end of the lesson whether you can sometimes read like this, for relaxation, instead of reading for relaxation in English.

Today, you are not asked to note down new words, unless you come across a phrase you know is going to be really useful to you. You may find that it is still helpful to read texts three times.

Some sources for reading materials – remember the order of difficulty – hardest at the top:

- Books written for French-speaking people your age
- Magazines written for French-speaking people your age
- Brochures and pamphlets without many pictures
- Brochures and pamphlets with lots of pictures
- Websites
- Books and magazines written for French-speaking people who can't read very well
- Books and magazines written for people learning French

If what you are reading seems too hard or too easy, move up or down the list. If you're having to use the dictionary for every other word, then it's too hard. If it's like reading in your own language, that's great, but you're probably not learning anything from it, so go up a level – unless you're at the top already – in which case, congratulations.

What is going on?

You may think you're just reading. It actually goes a lot deeper than that. In order to read, your subconscious mind is working hard. It's actually a bit like when you first learnt to read in your own language. You understand something consciously but you understand even more subconsciously. Your brain is busy decoding and sorting while you are relaxing. In fact, the more you relax, the better this all works.

But that isn't all.

As you read over and over repeated patterns, you learn those patterns. When you keep meeting the same new words they stop being new words. Your fluency in writing and speaking improves as you read. In fact, for fluency to improve you need to read.

Relaxed extensive reading is a very good way of:

- building up vocabulary
- increasing fluency
- increasing knowledge of grammar

Now make yourself a plan to do a fair amount of extensive reading over the next two weeks, and then review the plan at the end of the two weeks. How much can you comfortably fit in on a regular basis?

❋ **Reminder: Use the internet to help you with extensive reading.**

Aims and outcomes

To introduce students to the idea that reading in a foreign language can be as useful as reading in their own language.

Materials needed

- Student Sheet 40
- books and magazines written for French-speaking people of their age, brochures and pamphlets without many pictures, brochures and pamphlets with lots of pictures, websites, books and magazines written for French-speaking people who can't read very well and books and magazines written for people learning French
- internet access
- dictionaries

Classroom setup

Arrange tables for between four and six people. Explain that you might regroup them later. It can be a good idea to allow groups to work together on similar topics.

Hint

You might also consider making a tip sheet for them on note-taking. The Further Resources section may also be helpful.

Lesson starter (10 minutes)

Discuss the Student Sheet. Make sure they understand it. See if you can reorganize groups so that people are working together on similar topics. You may even consider allowing them to work towards presenting jointly.

Main lesson (30 minutes)

Allow the students to search through the materials, taking notes.

Plenary (15 minutes)

Remind students that they now have ten minutes to start organizing their materials. The remainder of the lesson and homework is for them to organize a presentation from the material they have found.

Homework (5 minutes)

Remind them that they are to finish organizing their presentations.

To make it harder

Ask the students to conduct their presentation in French.

To make it easier

Allow the students to present in English.

FURTHER RESOURCES

The following sites provide help with note-making:

Skills 4 Study *www.palgrave.com/skills4study/studyskills/reading/notes.asp*

Making Notes *www.thorns.info/skills/making_notes.htm*

Making Notes *www.doversherborn.org/doverelementary/Library/CANADA/MakingNotes.htm*

The following sites provide information about creating and using mindmaps:

Buzan World *www.buzanworld.com/Mind_Maps.htm*

Peter Russell *www.peterrussell.com/MindMaps/mindmap.php*

The Thinking Business *www.thethinkingbusiness.co.uk/mind_mapping_create.html*

Using mindmaps effectively

Mindmap Ideas *www.mind-mapping.co.uk/mind-maps-ideas.htm*

Mindmap Examples *www.mind-mapping.co.uk/mind-maps-examples.htm*

In this lesson you are going to learn how to use extensive reading in order to gather information for a presentation you will make about something you are interested in. You don't need to write words down separately in your vocabulary store, but you do need to make notes in French just as you do in English. You may later like to transfer those new words you meet to the list you intend to learn, but you don't need to do this today.

Today is about learning to use extensive reading materials to help you to make a presentation in French, or in English, on a topic that interests you.

Your topic

First, pick a topic you would like to find out about. For example:

A sport	A career you're interested in
A famous person	The French school system
A place in a French-speaking country	A French restaurant
An animal	Leisure activities for young people
One of your hobbies	Plan a holiday
A person from French history	Plan a day out

You may think of something else. Check with your teacher that it is acceptable. You will probably now be invited to work with other students who are working on a similar topic.

Which materials

Remember where you are with extensive reading and pick appropriate materials. The internet is likely to be particularly useful. You may find, as you all help each other, that you can extend your skill.

Making notes

You should now make notes about your topic as you sift through the material you find, just as you would if you were working in your own language. It is in fact considerably easier to make notes in French about French than it is to keep swapping languages. You may find making mindmaps particularly useful.

Pulling the material together (about 10 minutes before the end of the lesson)

Your teacher will tell you whether you will be making your presentation in French or in English. This will depend to some extent on how much work you have done on writing and speaking. You now need to sift through your notes and pull your presentation into some sort of shape. An outline made in French is useful, even if you are going to present eventually in English.

Homework

Polish up on your presentation. Consider using visuals or PowerPoint.

✳ Reminder: Revise parts of speech.

Aims and outcomes

To recap and remind the students of the opportunities for extensive reading and get them focused on making it part of what they do.

Materials needed

- Student Sheet 41
- extensive reading materials
- interactive whiteboard

Classroom setup

Students work individually at first and then with a partner. They may work with friends in this lesson.

Lesson starter (10 minutes)

Make sure that students understand the Student Sheet.

Main lesson

(25 minutes)

Students create their individual plans and begin to carry them out.

(10 minutes)

Students talk with a partner about what they intend to do and comment on each other's plans.

Plenary (10 minutes)

Collate students' ideas on the interactive whiteboard. Save for later revision sessions.

Homework (5 minutes)

Homework is to continue working on the plan and carry it out.

To make it harder

Ask student to share their action plan with their partners. Each student is responsible for checking that their partner is on schedule. They will agree on a date for meeting to discuss this.

To make it easier

In the plenary, create a generic action plan. Students use this one for homework.

FURTHER RESOURCES

Interactive whiteboard:

www.virtuallearning.org.uk/whiteboards/Learning_theories.pdf

http://findarticles.com/p/articles/mi_6950/is_/ai_n28452816

www.cilt.org.uk/14to19/ict/wikis/principles.htm

Extensive reading:

http://eltj.oxfordjournals.org/cgi/content/full/ccn041

http://eric.ed.gov/ERICWebPortal/custom/portlets/recordDetails/detailmini.jsp?_nfpb=true&_&ERICExtSearch_SearchValue_0= EJ759833&ERICExtSearch_SearchType_0=no&accno=EJ759833

http://nflrc.hawaii.edu/RFL/October2002/discussion/prowse.html

French books that are easy to read:

http://shop.linguascope.com/acatalog/Readers_French.html

www.younglinguists.com/languagebooks/subject/FRE/m4

Extensive Reading – Making the Most of your Opportunities

Extensive reading is about reading to get the gist of a text. Here are some different activities to do with extensive reading in French.

Reading for relaxation

Read in a relaxed way and you'll find it easier to understand texts. Enjoy this sort of reading. You will become more fluent as a result. You will pick up vocabulary as you go along without even noticing you're doing it. Make the most of any time your teacher allows for this and programme some of it into your own leisure time.

Reading for information

Read to find out things. You are more capable of doing this in French than you might at first think. You'll probably find that if you went around a French museum looking at the notices in French, you would gain more from this than looking at the English ones – and would understand more than you thought.

Reading as a vocabulary builder

Read about ten pages of text. Write down just one new word to learn from each page.

Where to find material – there are three main sources:

- what your teacher provides
- what your tandem partner can find for you
- what you find yourself when you go to a French-speaking country or what you find on a French website

Anything in print counts.

Levels

Remember the order of difficulty. Books written for French-speaking people your age, magazines written for French-speaking people your age, brochures and pamphlets without many pictures, brochures and pamphlets with lots of pictures, websites, books and magazines written for French-speaking people who can't read very well, books and magazines written for people learning French.

Your action plan

Work out a two-week action plan. Include:

- how much time you will spend on your reading
- when you will spend time on your reading
- how long you will stay on this level before you go up to the next one
- how you will acquire new materials
- how much time you will spend on each aspect of extensive reading
- a deadline within the two weeks for evaluating this action plan and setting up another long-term one

❊ Reminder: Spend some time on practising your role plays each week.

Language Skills 4: Writing

Aims and outcomes

To encourage students to make the most of the resources they have available and use what they know already to respond, in writing, to open-ended questions. This lesson does, of course, revisit a similar one for speaking.

Materials needed

- Student Sheet 42
- all available textbooks
- the students' own notes
- interactive whiteboard, if possible with a blank Student Sheet already loaded

Classroom setup

There should be four broad areas – two tables with eight students working at each.

Lesson starter (10 minutes)

Discuss the open-ended questions on the student sheet. Get students first to say what they can think of. Discuss some of the topics with them, noting down page numbers on the interactive whiteboard. If you have already completed the exercises on oral open-ended questions, you may already have some records of this. Use this as a starting point.

Main lesson (30 minutes)

Start different groups at different places, so that the class covers the whole range of topics. Allow the students to work through the open-ended questions, first writing down all that they can in their notebooks. They should then search for new material through the resources available.

Plenary (15 minutes)

Discuss the material they have found. Record it on the interactive whiteboard.

Homework (5 minutes)

Students carry on with this process, writing out answers as fully as possible.

To make it harder

Ask the students to write 200 words on one of the topics. They should write in full sentences as accurately as possible.

To make it easier

Complete one topic yourself before the lesson. Display this on the whiteboard and discuss this with the students before they start. Adjust the time of the lesson starter and main lesson to accommodate this.

FURTHER RESOURCES

French Topic Sheets *www.classroom-resources.co.uk/acatalog/Online_Catalogue_French_Topic_Sheets_1347.html* provides practice role play examples.

BBC Bitesize *www.bbc.co.uk/schools/gcsebitesize/french* provides topic-based revision in all skill areas.

French in a Click *http://frenchinaclick.com/frenchinaclick2008/topics.shtml* provides further practice in all skills on a variety of topics.

Answer these questions as fully as you can in your notebook. Then look through your books, your own notes and your resources to note down page numbers where you can get extra help with these questions.

If you have already done the open-ended oral questions, you might like to use that work as a starting point.

Tu peux décrire:

Ta famille	Ta maison
Ton collège	Ta ville/ton village
Ce que tu aimes faire dans ton temps libre	Ton ami(e)
Tes vacances l'année dernière	Ce que tu vas faire dans les grandes vacances
Ce que tu veux faire après le collège	Ce que tu as fait hier soir/le week-end dernier

You can also send these questions to your tandem partner. See what answers they come up with.

You should also plan how to finish the full answers over an appropriate period of time.

✳ Reminder: Spend some time on practising your spoken open-ended questions.

Open-ended Questions **STUDENT SHEET 42**

Aims and outcomes

To enable students to adapt work they read to write about themselves and to know what can easily be changed and what should be left alone.

Materials needed

- Student Sheet 43
- dictionaries
- interactive whiteboard, if possible with the first example on the Student Sheet already loaded

Classroom setup

Students should work individually during this lesson.

Lesson starter (20 minutes)

Discuss the first example. Create alternatives for the words in bold – note that they are mainly nouns and adjectives – and explain that these can be changed quite easily without having to change much of the structure, though students must be aware of agreements.

Main lesson

(10 minutes)

Let students find the words they can easily change on the second text.

(5 minutes)

Check these words with them

(10 minutes)

Let them try marking their second text.

Plenary (10 minutes)

Discuss their work with them and correct their answers. Make sure they understand the ideas.

Homework (5 minutes)

Students should attempt the third text for homework.

To make it harder

Ask the student to supply three suitable words for each word in bold.

To make it easier

Supply the students with a bank of words they might use, making sure there is at least one appropriate word for all of the words in bold on the Student Sheet.

FURTHER RESOURCES

Bubl Link *http://bubl.ac.uk/LINK/f/frenchlanguage.htm* provides many links to free language-learning resources.

1. Your teacher will show you how to make this text all about yourself. You will be changing mainly nouns (naming words) and adjectives (describing words). The words you should change are in **bold**. Some words in bold here are neither nouns nor adjectives. Do you have any idea why?

Il y a **cinq** personnes dans ma famille – **ma mère**, **mon père**, **mon frère** et **ma soeur**.

Ma mère s'appelle **Anne**. **Elle** a **quarante** ans. **Elle** est **grande** et **mince**. **Elle** a les cheveux **blonds**, **courts** et **frisés**. **Elle** travaille dans **un bureau**. Pendant son temps libre, **elle** aime **lire**.

Mon père s'appelle **Peter**. **Il** a **quarante-deux** ans. **Il** a les cheveux **courts** et **gris**. **Il** est **grand** et **mince**. **Il** est **pompier**. Pendant son temps libre **il** aime **regarder les matchs de football**.

Continue for other family members.

. . . Il va au college . . .

2. In the following passage, find the words you can change. Your teacher will discuss these with you later and give you some other words and phrases you could use.

J'habite Radcliffe. C'est une petite ville dans le nord d'Angleterre, près de Manchester. Il y a un marché, une boucherie, une bibliothèque, une banque, une boulangerie, une pharmacie, une piscine et un grand supermarché.

J'aime habiter Racliffe. Nous sommes près de la campagne et il faut seulement vingt minutes pour arriver au centre de Manchester.

Il y a beaucoup pour les jeunes gens. Il y un bon club de jeunes. Le week-end et le soir on peut aller en ville pour aller au ciné ou pour aller dans une boîte.

3. Now it's your turn to do it completely on your own. Adapt this passage to be about yourself.

Je vais au collège Brookfield. C'est un collège mixte pour les élèves de onze à seize ans. Il y a mille deux cents élèves et soixante-dix professeurs. Les bâtiments sont assez modernes. Il y a soixante-dix salles de classe, six laboratoires, une cantine, une salle de sports, un terrain de sports, quelques bureaux, une piscine et une bibliothèque.

Les cours commencent à huit heures quarante et finissent à quinze heures dix. Il y a deux recréations – à dix heures quarante à onze heures et à midi quarante jusqu'à une heure et demie. Les cours durent cinquante minutes.

J'adore les maths. Le professeur est très sympa. Les cours sont intéressants. Mais je déteste l'anglais. Le professeur est très stricte. Les cours sont ennuyeux.

Hint

Can you use what you have learnt here to help you to adapt your tandem partner's answer to questions from the last lesson?

✳ Reminder: **Spend some time learning words you have collected.**

Aims and outcomes

To take the students beyond cloning and adapting and awaken some grammar awareness in them.

Materials needed

- Student Sheet 44
- interactive whiteboard
- textbooks
- their own notes

Classroom setup

This is very much a teacher-led lesson. This may be the one time when you seat students alphabetically or boy-girl-boy-girl.

Hint

Create a wiki for all your groups who have done this exercise. Let the students post entries. You or your assistant or someone from your exchange school can correct entries.

Lesson starter (10 minutes)

Study the patterns with the students. Make sure that they understand what they are referring to. Point out that verbs change their form according to the person.

Main lesson (30 minutes)

Students study the recipe for a diary entry and attempt one of their own.

Plenary (15 minutes)

Build a diary entry with the class.

Allow students to work on their own. As they work, circulate, correcting and discussing work. Point out that they could try writing a diary entry every day and hand it in to be corrected, or they can ask their tandem partner to correct it.

Homework (5 minutes)

Students should attempt further diary entries on their own.

To make it harder

Ask the students from now on to write a diary entry every day. Put a strategy in place which allows these to be checked easily from time to time. You might consider involving the language assistant or the students' tandem partners.

To make it easier

Adjust the times for the main lesson and the plenary and build one or two extra diary entries with the whole class.

Look at the following patterns. Notice that they repeat: this can be very helpful but you can have more control over what you actually want to say if you know how to manipulate the pattern.

J'ai	mangé fait
Tu as	parlé visité regardé
Il/elle a	fini
Nous avons	choisi
vous avez	bu
ils/elles ont	vu

Je suis	allé(es)	tombé(es)
Tu es	arrivé(es)	monté(es)
Il/elle est	parti(es)	rentré(es)
Nous sommes	sorti(es)	
Vous êtes	entré(es)	
Ils/elles sont	descendu(es)	

Je me suis	réveillé(es)
Tu t'es	levé(es)
Il/elle s'est	lavé (es)
Nous nous sommes	douché(es)
Vous vous êtes	couché(es)
Ils/elles se sont	

Je	serai vendrai
Tu	auras parleras
Il/elle	fera visitera
Nous	mangerons verrons
Vous	arriverez visiterez
Ils/elles	finiront iront

Je vais	partir en vacances
Tu vas	regarder la télé
Il/elle va	aller en ville
Nous allons	faire des courses
Vous allez	aller au cinéma
Ils vont	manger dans un restaurant

Je	visitais
Tu	habitais
Il/elle	faisait beau/froid/du vent/du brouillard/chaud
Nous	allions
Vous	étiez
Ils/elles	avaient

Can you extend these patterns?

Recipe for a diary entry

Put down a few details about what you did today.

Reflect on something that went on – for example, what the weather was like.

Say what your plans are for tomorrow and further on in the future.

Hint

Don't say anything too personal – your teacher is going to correct this. Get your tandem partner to do the same. Then you'll have lots of good patterns to copy.

✳ Reminder: Rehearse your presentation.

Aims and outcomes

To encourage students to write competently and creatively, making the best use of what they already know or have easy access to.

Materials needed

- Student Sheet 45
- clipboards
- paper
- interactive whiteboard
- dictionaries
- students' notebooks
- digital cameras and/or mobile phones

Classroom setup

Allow students to work in friendship groups.

Hint

The first part of this lesson works very well if you complete it while out and about in a French-speaking country. The next best option is to take students out for a walk somewhere pleasant. Your own school grounds can be a surprisingly good venue. If all these fail, and the weather is lousy, you can either show them a DVD – *National Geographic* or French street scenes are appropriate – or ask the students to close their eyes and dig into a particular memory, especially a memory from a trip to a French-speaking country.

Lesson starter (10 minutes)

Discuss some useful vocabulary for whichever scenario you are using. Draw it out of the students but add in extras. If you are doing this on a trip in a French-speaking country, you may need to supply them with trigger vocabulary.

Main lesson

(20 minutes)

Experiencing the senses. Ask the student to write down what they can see, hear, feel, smell and taste. They must use words they know, but this can include words they know they've met before and forgotten. They may need to look them up again in notebooks or dictionaries when they're back in the classroom. If they are quite skilled at using dictionaries, about 10 per cent of the words may be ones that they can look up back in class.

If out and about in a French-speaking country they can include street signs and snippets of conversation they hear on the street. Can they also create French onomatopoeia? What noise does a French car or a French seagull make? This would also work quite well with a DVD of a French street scene.

(10 minutes)

Discuss with the students some of the ways in which they might write up their texts. See the Student Sheet. Use haikus and acrostic poems, for example.

Plenary (15 minutes)

Spend some time on explaining peer editing. Talk with the students about how they might perfect their texts.

Homework (5 minutes)

Students should craft their texts at home for a little longer. They can get you, the language assistant or their tandem partner to check their work later.

Hint

Consider putting the finished results on display – perhaps as a website, a blog or as a printed anthology. A student could be asked to design a cover.

Consider using Blogger *www.blogger.com* or Lightning Source *www.lightningsource.com*

To make it harder

Invite a native speaker of French to comment on the outcomes and discuss these comments with your students. Warn them before they begin the lesson that this will happen.

To make it easier

Consider providing the students with some 'starter' sheets of vocabulary. These could include a mixture of words and expressions they have already met and a few that they have not met that are very appropriate to the task.

1. Your teacher will discuss some special vocabulary with you for the area you are going to write in. Write this on something you can easily take with you. Can you add to this list? This exercise will prompt you to think of other things.

2. You are going to be taken on a walk somewhere, you are going to watch a film or you are going to be asked to visit something in your memory or imagination.

   You are asked to make notes on what you:

   - see
   - hear
   - smell
   - feel
   - taste

As you make notes remember:

   - they should be in French
   - they do only need to be notes – you can have single words or fragments of sentences
   - use only what you know, though you can also use what you know you have met but have temporarily forgotten
   - if there is something you really want to include, and you know you will be able to find it easily in a dictionary later, you can jot this down in English but this should not make up more than 10 per cent of the words you collect
   - if you are in a French-speaking country you will be surrounded by words you can hear or see

3. Back in the classroom, you will practise putting the language you have collected into a coherent form. In doing this, you should take notice of the sounds in the language. You might compose:

   - haikus – three lines of five, seven and five syllables with a slight change of direction in the last line
   - acrostic poems where you spell out a word as the first letter of each sentence
   - free verse/prose – you don't have to have full sentences and the words don't have to rhyme.

   Just put something together that works well.

4. Tell your partner two or three things you like about their work and two or three things they could improve. Point out any mistakes that you notice.

5. Perfecting your work. Get an expert – your teacher, your language assistant or your tandem partner – to check your work. Now work it up to publishable quality – for display, as part of a website or as part of a printed anthology.

✱ Reminder: Revise times, numbers and quantities.

Writing with the Senses   **STUDENT SHEET 45**

Aims and outcomes

To enable students to edit their own work, critique that of others and react positively to critique of their work by others.

Materials needed

- Student Sheet 46
- three pieces of each student's unedited work

Classroom setup

Students should work in twos, though one group of three is permissible.

Lesson starter (10 minutes)

Make sure students understand the Student Sheet. If your students have not yet done the grammar lessons, briefly discuss some common grammatical mistakes.

Main lesson

(10 minutes)

Students edit their own work.

(10 minutes)

Students read each other's work and give feedback.

(10 minutes)

Students react to their partner's critique and try to improve their work along the lines suggested.

Any students who finish early should try another piece of work.

Plenary (15 minutes)

Encourage students to carry on with this process on any remaining texts. Encourage them to find 'critique friends' and always use them as part of their editing process. Try to persuade them always to go through these stages of editing on any written work.

Homework (5 minutes)

Students should spend some more time on their texts, using friends' critiques to help them.

To make it harder

Ask students to make their critique in French. You may need to discuss some new vocabulary with them so that they can do this.

To make it easier

Limit self-critique and peer-critique to just three items. Make sure that students understand that just because only three items have been commented on, the rest of the text is not necessarily accurate.

FURTHER RESOURCES

French Grammar *www.french-linguistics.co.uk/grammar* provides many exercises and explanations about French grammar.

About French *http://french.about.com/library/begin/bl_begin_gram.htm* provides tips on French grammar. Parts of speech are explained.

French Verbs *http://french.about.com/library/weekly/bltopicsub-g.htm* on French grammar.

Real French *www.realfrench.net/index.php* is hosted by Manchester Metropolitan University and gives more tips about grammar and other aspects of learning French.

French Links *www.realfrench.net/index.php* provides more grammar tips.

Buxton Online *www.buxtononline.net/french-tuition/grammar.htm* demystifies French grammar.

1. First of all, edit your work yourself. Edit for one thing at a time.

   a Does the piece have overall structure? Is there a definite beginning, structured middle and an end?

   b Does the content develop in a satisfactory way?

   c Have you included the right combination of 'show-off factors'? Have you used a mixture of tenses? Have you included some good joining words?

   d Do a grammatical check. If you've covered all the grammar lessons, you'll know exactly what to do. If not, just be aware of some of the things that your teacher tells you. Normally for grammar, you should do the following checks:

   - verbs – for tense, person, voice and mood
   - word order
   - parts of speech
   - use of prepositions
   - numbers and gender
   - your own personal common mistakes

   e Finally check for overall flow. This is best done by reading aloud.

   So, potentially, you have checked your work eleven times.

2. Now ask a friend to comment on your work. Allow them to make notes on your work. They should note in anything at all that they notice. You do the same for them. You should then each name three things that work well in the text; three things that are not so good; and make three recommendations about what your partner could do to improve their work.

3. React to what your partner has said. You don't have to do as they suggest, but you might consider their suggestions. Often, another person can point out that something is not working. If you do not like their suggestion it may be possible to find an alternative.

   You do need to learn to see any criticism as being helpful rather than a judgement about yourself. Your friends and your teacher, the language assistant or your tandem partner can all be very helpful.

Further work

Now try to get into the habit of checking all of your written work this way.

Hint

Ask your tandem partner to be your editing friend. You can help each other.

How will you react to what your teacher or the language assistant eventually says about your work?

❄ **Reminder: Rehearse your presentation for your oral exam.**

Aims and outcomes

To enable students to learn from work that has been corrected.

Materials needed

- Student Sheet 47
- students' corrected work
- an example of corrected work on the interactive whiteboard, and examples of some work to be corrected

Classroom setup

Students will work individually at first and then with people sitting near them. This is another teacher-led lesson, so seat students in a way that minimizes disruption.

Hint

It is a good idea to standardize your way of marking and share your methods with your students.

You need to distinguish between marking and correcting. Correcting is formative. Marking is summative. One argument for correcting every mistake is that it prevents students from learning incorrect patterns. A further argument says you should not make corrections in red. Green is a better choice. It is easier on the eyes yet shows up against blue/black ink and print.

Arguments in *Higher Education* also go against awarding a mark. The reason is that students tend to only look at the mark rather than the comments. You can, however, train students to take the comments on board. The mark can be useful in setting a standard. But do you award that mark against a final goal – for example, how good is this compared to a piece of GCSE Higher Writing? Or how good is this piece of work against the expectations that the teacher has now? Do you want to give a separate mark for effort? You need to be clear about this and how it fits with your institution's marking policy and you need to make sure your students understand this also.

Summative comments are useful: you might consider starting with the positives and saying what works about the piece. Then highlight the weaknesses that, if eliminated, would make the biggest difference to the effectiveness of the piece. Finally, give the student three targets that are easy to achieve.

When correcting grammar you might consider pointing out the mistake but not giving the student the correction, especially if you have already completed the grammar lessons with the class.

You might consider students submitting work electronically and correcting electronically. Students can then quickly produce a 'clean' copy. But they should still keep the corrected one. If using Microsoft Word, you can use the Track Changes function.

Lesson starter (15 minutes)

Make sure that students understand the Student Sheet.

Main lesson (30 minutes)

Discuss the corrections on the piece already on the interactive whiteboard, and then correct a second piece with the students.

Plenary (10 minutes)

Explain how students should continue work on their own corrected pieces. Discuss getting into a routine and why they should always do this.

Homework (5 minutes)

Students are to study their own corrected pieces.

To make it harder

Ask students to keep a log of the type of mistakes they make. They should look thorough this log from time to time.

To make it easier

Ask students to provide work in Microsoft Word. Use Track Changes to correct work. Ask the student to comment on the first three changes they encounter. Make sure they are familiar with the functions of Track Changes.

Look at the work your teacher has corrected and marked. You will have all or some of the following.

Grades

Perhaps one for effort and one for achievement. What is this grade telling you? Does this reflect a grade you would get for the same piece of work in an exam? Or does it represent how well you have completed the task? Make sure you understand the meaning of the grade.

Positive comments

Your teacher is telling you what you have done right. Be proud of this and remember to do it again next time.

Comments about weaknesses

Make sure you understand this and work out what you can do to avoid it in the future. Remember this is not a criticism of you but a tool to help you do even better next time.

Targets

Make sure you understand these. Try to remember them and follow them.

Spelling corrections

These may be marked just 'sp'. There may well be many of them. Choose up to five – perhaps the words that you think will be most useful to you in the future. Write each one out five times.

Grammar corrections

Your teacher may not have corrected the grammar, but may just tell you what type of mistake it is. This is the code they use:

Vt	verb tense
Vp	verb person
Vv	verb voice
Vm	verb mood
Wo	word order
Pr	preposition
Pos	part of speech
Ag	agreement

And also, this is not really grammar but you may do the corrections in a similar way:

U   usage, i.e. it works grammatically but it's not actually what they do in French. Just think about the unusual way French people count, for example

M   meaning – you've used the wrong word; this sometimes happens because you've been unlucky when using a dictionary.

If they have not corrected the sentences for you, try to correct all of them. You may do this over several sessions if there are many. Don't worry, you can make a lot of mistakes – French people do make the same sort of mistakes – and you also make similar ones in English but can still get a good mark. Look through some corrected work before you start a new piece of written work.

✳ **Reminder: Practise writing with patterns.**

Vocabulary Building

Aims and outcomes

To enable students to collect language in a way that is enjoyable and that makes maximum use of what they have collected.

Materials needed

- Student Sheet 48
- vocabulary books or other vocabulary storage devices
- all sorts of materials – all their textbooks, reading materials, loaded computer terminals – anything interesting in French
- interactive whiteboard

Classroom setup

Students should work in groups of four to six, around a table full of stimulating materials, but should still be able to see the whiteboard.

Lesson starter (10 minutes)

Make sure students understand the Student Sheet.

Main lesson (30 minutes)

Allow them to collect language. Make it a bit of a treasure hunt: who can find the most interesting word or phrase?

Plenary (15 minutes)

Students each have a turn at using their key phrase meaningfully.

Homework (5 minutes)

Students spend time on learning vocabulary and considering how they can get a vocabulary habit up and running.

To make it harder

Ask the students to adopt collecting words as an open-ended habit. There is no limit to this, though they should use the common sense rules discussed on the Student Sheet.

To make it easier

Make an agreement with the students about how many words they will collect – perhaps three every French lesson – until they feel that they would like to take this further.

FURTHER RESOURCES

About French *http://french.about.com/library/begin/bl_begin_vocab.htm* provides topic-based vocabulary lists.

French Today *www.frenchtoday.com/vocabulary* provides an interactive way of learning vocabulary.

Syvum *www.syvum.com/learn/vocabulary/French* provides quizzes on vocabulary.

Acquiring French vocabulary *www.utm.edu/staff/globeg/vocab.shtml* gives advice on how to learn vocabulary.

Quizz Tree *www.quiz-tree.com/French_Vocabulary_main.html* provides free quizzes on French vocabulary.

Indo European Language *www.ielanguages.com/french.html* provides a tutorial on learning vocabulary.

Where you can get words

You can collect words from the following places:

- when you are out and about in a French-speaking country
- from your teacher, language assistant, or tandem partner
- work you do in class
- anything else you read
- work you have had corrected

Some thoughts about collecting and learning language

- It is a silly waste of a valuable resource if you never write down vocabulary
- It is tedious and a silly waste of your time to write down absolutely every new word you come across
- It is a silly waste of your time if you write down tons of words and never learn any of them
- It is probably impossible to learn every single word you write down
- Some words you need to know actively, some words you need to know passively
- These sentences do not necessarily contradict each other, but you do need to make some decisions

Collect delightful words and phrases

These words and phrases take you by surprise and delight you. They really are absolutely made for you. You love them. Write each such phrase down and learn it, then make sure you use it actively within three days. Using it actively makes it stick.

You often find these words and phrases when you're not actually looking, but if you do find one, treasure it. Today you are going to deliberately look for one. You may find more than one. Then you're going to use one on your classmates.

Learning the rest

Try this.

Set your work out in four columns: French   English   French   English

Cover the English and test yourself.

Put a pencil mark by each one you get wrong.

Keep retesting and rubbing pencil marks out until you get them all right.

Then do the same for English to French.

Reward yourself when you have completed a page.

Every twenty pages or so go back and do an old page.

Set aside time each day or week for doing this. Let it become a habit like cleaning your teeth.

✳ **Reminder: Try some extensive reading – read something written for French-speaking people and don't worry about understanding every word.**

Aims and outcomes

To illustrate the advantages and disadvantages of using a bilingual dictionary and to demonstrate how to use it effectively.

Materials needed

- dictionaries – try to have as many different examples available as possible
- Student Sheet 49

Classroom setup

Students should work individually and be heavily guided by the teacher, so seat the students for minimum disruption. At the end of the lesson you can form the students into four teams.

Lesson starter

(10 minutes)

Explain the 'elephant in the room rule' – the first point on the Student Sheet. Sometimes, because you use a dictionary, you serendipitously come across an unusual word or expression. Students should shout out whenever this happens to them in the lesson – but of course they should not get silly. Consider having some sort of reward ready for them. Discuss the opening comments on the Student Sheet.

Main lesson

(10 minutes)

Complete the alphabetic exercise on the Student Sheet. Make sure the exercise is clear. Allow the students to complete it.

Answers Students should have put the words into the following order: Arrièrre, artifice, bouillir, bouillon, chequer, cruche, daim, dais, force, forcé, forcément, fruit, irreparable, mon, mur, pourcentage, retardé, voyante

(10 minutes)

Complete the 'Find These Words' exercise. Make sure the exercise is clear. Allow the students to complete it.

Answers (1) petite cuillère, (2) cadron solaire, (3) jour de semaine, (4) ragoût de boeuf, (5) fauteuil, (6) journal du dimanche, (7) uniforme scolaire, (8) déjeuner à la cantine scolaire, (9) argent de poche, (10) livre de bibliothèque

(10 minutes)

Complete the 'Oh whoops' exercise. Make sure the exercise is clearly understood. Allow the students to complete it.

Answers (1) bouchon, (2) tronc, (3) gras, (4) rouler sur la piste, (5) casser les pieds à, (6) fulminer, (7) réserver, (8) plomb, (9) harceler (10) animal de compagnie

Plenary (15 minutes)

Have a dictionary looking-up race. Form the students into four teams for this exercise.

Answers (1) memory, remember, (2) kid, (3) scatterbrain, mad, (4) get a tan, (5) surroundings, (6) go up in flames, (7) unexpected, (8) buyer, (9) fuss, (10) sheaf

Homework (5 minutes)

Students should create similar exercises to the above for their classmates.

To make it harder

Ask students to write a guide for younger students about how to use a bilingual dictionary.

To make it easier

Extend the plenary and create one exercise with the class. Record it on the whiteboard.

Treasure hunt (or 'there's an elephant in the room')

Sometimes, when you're using the dictionary, you come across a peach of a word. This may well happen in today's lesson. This is the one time in your school life when you are allowed to hoot and shout and trumpet like an elephant and let the rest of the group know.

Comments about using French–English dictionaries

- It can make you very lazy.
- It is a good way of collecting new words.
- There are lots of traps.
- It is more useful for finding out what French words mean than for finding new French words.
- If you have a dictionary you can do anything.
- It is the best aid to language learning that there is.

Alphabetical order

This is always important and may seem easy but it's not always as easy as you think. Put the following words into alphabetical order:

buillir	cruche	irreparable	voyante	daim
bouillon	force	mur	mon	chequer
arrièrre	forcement	pourcentage	fruit	
artifice	forcé	retardé	dais	

Find these words

(These double-barrelled words may be listed under one part or the other, e.g. for 1. you might look up 'tea' or 'spoon').

1. teaspoon	4. beef stew	7. school uniform	10. library book
2. sundial	5. armchair	8. school dinner	
3. weekday	6. Sunday paper	9. pocket money	

Oh whoops

Sometimes words in either language have more than one meaning. A good way of checking is to look them up the other way round, i.e. first English to French, then French to English. Try these:

1. jam (traffic)	4. taxi (what aircraft does)	7. book (make a reservation)	10. pet (animal you keep for company)
2. trunk (of tree)		8. lead (metal)	
3. bold (font)	5. bug (annoy)	9. dog (pester)	
	6. storm (be angry)		

Looking-up race

See which team can find the meaning of these words the quickest:

1. souvenir	3. étourdi	5. alentours	7. imprévu	9. tralala
2. marmot	4. brunir	6. cramer	8. preneur	10. gerbe

✳ **Reminder: Keep on collecting new words.**

Aims and outcomes

To show students that they can be creative with language at the same time as actually forcing themselves to meet and use new words.

Materials needed

- Student Sheet 50
- dictionaries
- pictures where one colour is dominant
- postcard-sized pieces of scrap paper
- photocopies of appendices pages 189 and 190 or link provided to the Continuum Companion website

Classroom setup

Set up red, blue, yellow, green, black and white tables. Explain to the class before you let them into the room that they should look at the pictures on the desks as they go in and sit themselves down at the desk with pictures that most appeal to them. If that table is already full, they should just quietly seek another. All colours are of equal value.

Lesson starter (15 minutes)

Work with the colour 'violet'. Get the students to shout out in French, words they associate with that colour. Encourage them to use the dictionary to look up new ones. When you have about 30 words, show the students how to form the words into haikus. The general principles are:

- three lines
- line 1 has five syllables
- line 2 has seven syllables
- line 3 has five syllables
- there is a change in mood/content in last line
- there should be a strong image of nature in the haiku – but as we all belong to nature, practically anything meets this

Encourage the students to go for what they like the sound of.

Main lesson

(15 minutes)

Give out Student Sheet 50. Make sure students understand the instructions. Starting with what they know, but this time moving rapidly on to using dictionaries, students are to write down words to do with the colour on scrap paper, putting them into the middle of their table as they work.

(15 minutes)

Students form haikus from the words they have collected. They can add in extra bits. They should write up any that work well. Warn them three minutes before the end that they should write up at least one.

Plenary (10 minutes)

Have fun getting the students to read out their haikus.

Homework (5 minutes)

Set the Student Sheet as homework.

To make it harder

Ask the students to produce haikus on three new topics, none of which should be colours.

To make it easier

Discuss a haiku on a topic other than colour and put it on the whiteboard before students start working individually.

You are going to build some haikus to do with colours using your English–French dictionary to help you.

1. Use a different colour from the one you used in class earlier. Look up as many words and expressions as you can. You might write them on separate sheets of paper or you can collect them in a Word document on your computer.

2. Form some haikus.

   The general principles are that there are:

   • three lines

   • line 1 has five syllables

   • line 2 has seven syllables

   • line 3 has five syllables

   • there is a change in mood/content in last line.

   • there should be a strong image of nature in the haiku – but as we all belong to nature, practically anything meets this

   • go for what sounds good.

3. Write out a selection of your best haikus. Remember to note down any 'elephants' you come across, but there's no need to make a separate note of them if you are including them in the haiku.

4. Try to learn some of your haikus by heart. You might consider making a display of them around your house, or your classroom, or creating a mini website or blog of them. You could even consider asking your parents or teacher to have them made into postcards, mouse mats, T-shirts, calendars or mugs. Try *www.vistaprint.co.uk* or *www.cafepress. co.uk* Alternatively, you can just make bookmarks in a Word document. Your teacher will give you the templates and instructions or you can visit the Continuum Companion website.

5. Now think of another topic about which to do haikus – perhaps seasons or places. Work through the same stages. Do make sure you show them to someone – a friend, family, your teacher, the language assistant or your tandem partner. Have fun!

Hint

Consider creating haikus for every topic you do in French. It's a fun way to build up and learn vocabulary.

We have now learnt about many skills and habits that help our language learning. Take a few moments now to see whether you have the right balance of these. Are there any more areas you need to spend more time on? Go back to the mindmaps we made at the beginning.

❈ Reminder: Have a go at adapting a role play situation. Change some of the vocabulary.

Aims and outcomes

To give students further practice at being creative while simultaneously gathering new vocabulary, this time in a more personal way.

Materials needed

- Student Sheet 51
- a dictionary for every student
- interactive whiteboard

Classroom setup

Students should work individually but present their work to others at the end.

Lessons starter (15 minutes)

Write your own name or that of a well-known personality – perhaps local – on the board vertically in large letters. e.g.:

G

I

L

L

J

A

M

E

S

Students should suggest words that begin with each letter. They may use dictionaries.

Main lesson (30 minutes)

Now ask the students to arrange the words into an order that sounds right to them. They can construct sentences if they wish: this is particularly useful if a letter repeats – as it does in the example. These poems work well also if a whole sentence is included between two-thirds and four-fifths of the way through.

Students should then try writing their own poem. Note that instructions are on the Student Sheet.

Plenary (10 minutes)

Students share their work.

Homework (5 minutes)

Note that there are further suggestions on the Student Sheet, which can be used for homework.

To make it harder

Ask students to think of three more topics on which they could write acrostic poems.

To make it easier

Discuss with students three more topics on which they could write acrostic poems. Then provide them with the three new words.

1. On a sheet of A4 paper, write your name vertically, spreading the letters evenly over the page. Make a box for each letter, e.g.:

G

I

L

L

J

A

M

E

S

Use your dictionary to find as many appropriate words for each letter as you can. This is the one time you should use your dictionary randomly – perhaps even more so than you did for writing the haikus. Note you are not thinking in English. You are working directly with French.

2. Arrange your words for best effect. Just use your instinct. If you have a repeating letter, you might consider using a full sentence. These poems work well if they have at least one full sentence as well as a random selection of words and phrases. It is good if that sentence comes between two-thirds and four-fifths of the way through the poem.

3. You will be asked in class to read out your work. If you've managed more than one, choose your best. Think about making items with your poems, as you did with your haikus. For bookmarks, just use one word for each letter, and set up your page as 'landscape', then cut them into shape.

4. For homework, you are asked to do another couple of acrostic poems. You could choose another person, a place, or one of the topics you are studying in French.

Hint

Do you not have a dictionary yet or would you like to acquire a second one?

Think of the advantages and disadvantages of the following:

- a small one that fits into a pocket or a handbag

- the next size up from this

- a free online one

- one you can load on to your computer

- a really big one you could not carry about with you

✳ Reminder: Have a go at extending a role play. Add in another dramatic element.

Aims and outcomes

To demonstrate to students how they can use their tandem/exchange partner to help them to build up vocabulary.

Materials needed

- Student Sheet 52
- lots of pictures – go for busy ones; they can be from anywhere – scrounge magazines from friends, family, neighbours and colleagues
- it is good to do this lesson 'live' with your exchange school, who may well like to do a 'mirror' lesson on their side
- internet enabled computers
- scanners

Classroom setup

Students will work individually – it is ideal if they can work in a room with internet-enabled computers. If you do not have one computer per student, you will need to set up a system that guarantees fair usage.

Sort the pictures into piles so that each student has six or so, as varied as possible.

Lesson starter (10 minutes)

Set up classroom rules and etiquette. Make sure students understand the Student Sheet.

Main Lesson (35 minutes)

Students complete the exercises on the Student Sheet. As they work, you may wish to discuss the outcomes of each exercise and any snags they meet.

Plenary (10 minutes)

Discuss outcomes and snags in more detail. Allow some of the students to share their work.

Homework (5 minutes)

Complete homework as described on the Student Sheet.

To make it harder

Ask students to actively use ten of the new words they meet today in a piece of writing or while speaking.

To make it easier

Provide students with an already marked-up picture as a model.

Here are some ideas for how you can work effectively with your tandem/exchange partner to help build up your vocabulary.

1. Using pictures

From the pile of pictures, select the most interesting. Clearly label objects, people and places on it with a number. Scan the photo and email it to your partner; in the body of the email ask them to fill in the names for these objects, people and places in French. When you get your picture and list back, just file them away safely together. You can test yourself on vocabulary later by just looking at the list of words (French to English), then by just looking at the picture (English to French).

Of course, it is only polite that you should now fill in a picture for them – perhaps the same one?

2. Looking at the space around you

Look around you in the classroom. Look at the room, the people in it and the computer you are working on. In English write a list of 20 words that you do not know the French for. You can include colours and other adjectives. You might also include words about your feelings.

Set your work out so that when you get your words back from your partner, it is already neatly organized in two or four columns. Email this to your partner.

Do you realize that this is as good for their passive vocabulary as it is for your active vocabulary?

3. Using your imagination

Think of one of the topics you are studying in French. Pick your weakest one. Imagine a scene within this topic. Write down 20 words and phrases in English that you do not know in French. You might find it useful to focus on the senses: what do you see, hear, feel (in both senses of the word) taste and smell?

Again write or type this neatly so that it is ready for learning when you come back.

Again, this is as good for your partner as it is for you.

Hint

Do you want to store this vocabulary in a separate ring binder? Or perhaps even electronically? If you're using a school computer, do you want to email this to yourself at home?

Homework

Spend one hour on a combination of the following activities:

- working more with your tandem partner on these exercises
- working out a useful routine for acquiring and learning this type of material
- working out the best way of storing this work
- beginning your routine.

✳ Reminder: Do some general revision on role plays. Work with a partner.

Aims and outcomes

To demonstrate yet another way of gaining vocabulary that takes the student beyond the limitations of the exam syllabus and the school textbook.

Materials needed

- Student Sheet 53
- scrap paper, pens and pencils
- suitable outdoor clothing
- dictionaries
- if possible, a link with your tandem school for the second half of the lesson
- the language assistant, if possible
- this lesson can easily be adapted for use on a class trip to a French-speaking country and for the student to use individually when they are on an exchange visit. It is ideally conducted mainly outdoors. You may wish to take the students off-site for 20 minutes, so will need to complete appropriate formalities, such as getting permission and completing a risk assessment. It may well be useful to have other adults with you so that there is one adult per six students. It will be even better if they are French speakers.

Classroom setup

Allow students to work in friendship groups of four to six.

Lesson starter (10 minutes)

Set up safety features. Make sure that students understand what they need to do. They should take with them appropriate outdoor clothing, pens and scrap paper. Give out Student Sheet 53.

Main lesson

(20 minutes)

You take a walk in your chosen environment. Every four minutes stop for one minute and get the students to record words in English that they don't know the French for. Note that many of the students will have the same words: this will be important later.

(15 minutes)

Students work collaboratively and with their tandem partners and the language assistant to find out the French for as many words that they have in English as they can. You might consider getting students to type these up into documents in a shared space so that they can later be printed out for each student.

Plenary (10 minutes)

Allow students to share their work with the rest of the group.

Homework (5 minutes)

See the Student Sheet.

Variations:

On a French street

This works very well. Students gather so much more because they are surrounded by French and because of the words already supplied in sign language. Try to minimize delay between their gathering words and adding in the French. Consider allowing a mixture of French and English.

On exchange

Your students can complete this privately with their exchange partners. It can be reciprocal. One good method is to use the walk to school each day. They can even get into testing each other this way.

To make it harder

Give the students a high limit on the number of words they have to collect today.

To make it easier

Provide the students with a sheet on which there are already a few words in English that are common in your chosen environment. Alternatively, you may create such a list with the students before they set out.

The walk

You can do this exercise any time, but today you will do it with your classmates.

You are going to take a walk in groups of four to six people for about 20 minutes. About once every five minutes you will be asked to jot down in English all the objects, people, places, colours you see, hear, taste, smell and feel (in both senses of the word) that you can think of in one minute.

It's okay to shout out, since you'll be working with other people in your group, and in fact it's even likely that there will be a lot of overlap between you and the other people in your class.

Back in the classroom

You now have 15 minutes with your classmates and possibly the help of your teacher, the language assistant, your tandem partner and dictionaries to write down as many of these words you can in French. Your teacher will advise you on how to do this. This is a whole class exercise and you are all going to benefit from each other's work.

If you do this at another time on your own, you can send your list to your tandem partner for help.

Homework

You need to spend an hour on a combination of the following activities:

- completing your list of words
- learning your list of words
- working out a routine for getting this type of vocabulary-building into your work routines
- consider the tips on working with an exchange partner and working while in a French-speaking country
- working out your routine

Working in a French-speaking country

This works especially well when you are in a French-speaking country. You might at this point record a mixture of French and English words. There will be a small delay between when you collect the words and when you can write them up and learn them.

Working with your exchange partner while on an exchange

You can work together on this, helping each other in several areas. Consider using the journey to and from school each day to add more words to each other's vocabulary and also to test each other. But do leave some time for just chatting!

Hint

Revisit some of the ideas about how to learn new words from previous lessons.

❖ Reminder: Study your personal oral questions again.

Grammar Building

Aims and outcomes

To familiarize students with the purpose of grammar, to give them an understanding of the difference between grammar and usage – and that the latter is also important – and provide an overview of what it entails.

Materials needed

- Student Sheet 54
- interactive whiteboard
- textbooks

Classroom setup

Set out the tables so that students can see the whiteboard, and so that they are in at least six groups. Each group should have a quantity of the textbooks on their table. The students should work in mixed-ability groups – lower with middle and middle with higher – and you should take ability within groups into account when setting up tasks later.

Lesson starter (15 minutes)

Tell students to name things they see and make short statements in phrases about them, but no full sentences. Write what they are saying on the board.

You may end up with something like 'window broken boy ball near computer tell caretaker glass floor quickly ran away mess desk rain'.

What could that possibly be about? Has the caretaker broken the computer or has the boy broken the window? Has a glass of water been spilt? Point out that it is the use of grammar that makes this clear.

Discuss the difference between grammar and usage. Grammar makes meaning clear. Usage is just what we really do – sometimes not all that logically.

Discuss the mindmap on the Student Sheet. Make clear as many grammatical terms as you can. Work from the centre outwards. Students should take notes as you go along.

Main lesson (30 minutes)

Start each group off with one of the six main grammar points on the mindmap on the Student Sheet. Note that number, time and quantities have been included even though strictly speaking they are usage rather than grammar. Students should scour their textbooks and jot down the page numbers where help on each point can be found.

Plenary (10 minutes)

Get the groups to give feedback.

Homework (5 minutes)

Make sure they understand the homework task described on the Student Sheet.

To make it harder

Alter the lesson order slightly and let the students decide what the different points of grammar are.

To make it easier

Limit students to finding three areas they understand well and three they find more difficult. Explain that they will meet the rest in the next few weeks.

Further work

Study the mindmap you have looked at in class. Which are your weakest areas? Make a plan for how you are going to bring them all up to scratch. Beware, though, that there will be separate lessons on verbs and tenses, verbs and person, verbs and voice, verbs and mood, word order, prepositions, parts of speech, gender, number and times and numbers and quantities

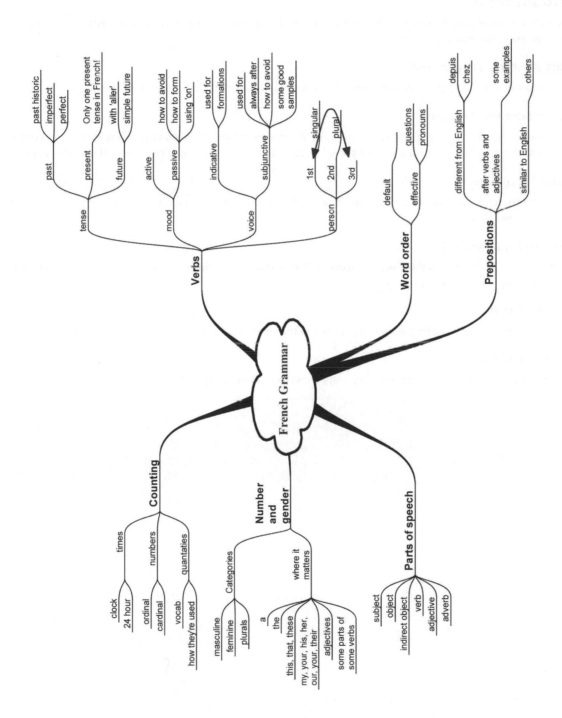

❊ **Reminder: Take a piece of written French and have a go at cloning and adapting it – just replace some items of vocabulary.**

Aims and outcomes

To increase students' understanding and knowledge of tense, to show them that it is possible to learn all they need to know about tense quite quickly and to get them into the habit of practising regularly.

Materials needed

- Student Sheet 55
- interactive whiteboard
- dictionaries
- textbooks

Classroom setup

This lesson is quite heavily teacher-led, with some individual work by students. Seat students to enable most effective communication and concentration.

Lesson starter (15 minutes)

Make sure students understand past, present and future tenses referred to on the Student Sheet.

Main lesson (30 minutes)

Ask them to write a few sample past tense sentences. Write a few coherent ones on the board, which may perhaps later form a story. Do the same for future and present tenses. Encourage them to piece together a story themselves as they go along.

Plenary (10 minutes)

Have some students read out their story. Discuss possibility of now writing a daily diary if students are not already doing this (see the Student Sheet).

Homework (5 minutes)

Students should start writing the diary as discussed. They should aim to do ten minutes a day. Perhaps they can write about four to five days for the first entry.

To make it harder

Ask the students to try reporting on what happened in their favourite sitcom during the last episode.

To make it easier

Extend the plenary and write a generic diary entry with the students on the whiteboard.

In any piece of writing, try to use a variety of these tenses.

Past

Perfect with 'avoir'	with être	reflexives	Imperfect
J'ai mangé	je suis allé(e)	je me suis réveillé(e)	j'habitais
tu as bu	tu es venu(e)	tu t'es levé(e)	tu dormais
il a nagé	il est entré	il s'est lavé	il faisait
ell a pris	elle est sortie	elle s'est habillée	elle avait
nous avons dormi	nous sommes monté(e)s	nous nous sommes déshabille(e)s	nous étions
vous avez fini	vous êtes descendu(e)s	vous vous êtes dépeché(e)s	vous auriez
ils ont vendu	ils sont devenus	ils se sont rasés	ils allaient
elles ont parlé	elles sont nées	elles se sont douchées	elles mangeaient
	(plus a few more)	(plus a few more)	

Past historic – you meet this one in books.   Pluperfect 'had' – imperfect of avoir/être plus verb

Present tense

Hooray! Only one in French . . . but three different types of verb . . . and all the exceptions.

je	parle	finis	vends
tu	parles	finis	vends
il/elle	parle	finit	vend
nous	parlons	finissons	vendons
vous	parlez	finissez	vendez
ils/elles	parlent	finissent	vendent

But even these seem to form a pattern after a while. Try to learn a few each week.

Future

Aller + infinitve		simple future	conditional
Je vais	manger	je mangerai	je mangerais
Tu vas	finir	tu finiras	tu firniais
Il va	vendre	il vendra	il vendrait
Nous allons	aller	nous vendrons	nous vendrions
Vous allez	courir	vous courrez	vous courriez
Ils vont	pouvoir	ils pourront	ils pourraient

There are a few more irregular future stems.

WRITE A LITTLE EVERY DAY IN A VARIETY OF TENSES.

❄ Reminder: Use your dictionary to build up your vocabulary.

Aims and outcomes

To introduce students to easy ways of changing the 'person' in a verb.

Materials needed

- Student Sheet 56
- grammar books and verb tables
- interactive whiteboard

Classroom setup

Students will work part of the time closely with the teacher, and part of the time in groups of four. They should be able to see the board at all times.

Lesson starter (15 minutes)

Discuss all of the exercises.

Main lesson (30 minutes)

Students work though the exercises in their groups of four.

Plenary (10 minutes)

Correct the sentences from exercises 1–3 with the students, writing answers on the whiteboard. If there is time, listen to some of their answers to exercise 4.

Homework (5 minutes)

Students should write another version of exercise 4.

To make it harder

Ask the students to write a short story about 200 words long for a French-speaking child.

To make it easier

Extend the plenary and play a team game. Give the students a sentence and another person. They gain points by correctly changing the person.

Exercise 1

When you answer a question addressed to you, you usually have to change the form of the verb from the 'tu' or 'vous' (second person) form to the 'je' (first person) form.

You have to recognize the tense and then change the verb accordingly. You might need to refer to work you have already done on verbs.

Try these:

1. Quel âge as-tu?

2. Où habites tu?

3. Es-tu déjà allée en France?

4. Que feras-tu pendant les grandes vacances?

5. Qu'est-ce qu tu vas faire en septembre?

Try to make up five more questions of your own.

Exercise 2

It's often easier if you are talking about he, she or they (third person) but watch out for open-ended questions like those below. In fact, with open-ended questions, try to give a three-part answer – or longer, if you can. Be careful where you need an agreement.

Try these:

1. Que fera Jean demain?

2. Qu'est-ce que Janine et Annette ont fait hier soir?

3. Qu'est-ce Jean et Pierre font d'habitude le samedi?

4. Que fait ton père le week-end?

5. Qu'est-ce qu ta mère a fait le week-end dernier

Exercise 3

The 'vous' (second person) form can represent speaking to one person or to two or more. Try the following questions. Answer them twice – first as if they refer to one person and second as if referring to several people (so you are using 'we' – 'nous', i.e. second person plural). Notice the mixture of tenses.

1. Où allez-vous en vacances?

2. Qu'est-ce que vous y ferez?

3. Qu'est-ce que vous aimez faire le week-end?

4. Que faîtes-vous le soir?

5. Qu'est-ce que vous avez fait le week-end dernier?

Exercise 4

If you're talking about more than one person, you need to use 'ils' or 'elles' (third person plural). Note if the crowd is mixed, you use 'ils' – even if there are six girls and only one boy.

Now write a short passage about what four friends – two boys and two girls – did on holiday.

Hint

Whenever you write a passage of French, try to use a mixture of tenses and persons – i.e. je (first person singular), tu (second person singular familiar), il/elle/on (third person singular), vous (second person plural and singular polite), nous (first person plural) and ils/elles (third person plural).

❋ **Reminder: Revise your verb tenses.**

Verbs – Person

STUDENT SHEET 56

Aims and outcomes

To introduce the students to the concept of voice and show them how they can and why they should avoid the passive, but also to show them when they cannot avoid it and how to form it. They will also be introduced to 'on'.

Materials needed

- Student Sheet 57
- textbooks
- dictionaries containing verb tables
- interactive whiteboard

Classroom setup

This is largely a teacher-led lesson, though students may complete the exercises in pairs. Seat students so that they face you and the interactive whiteboard, where answers to the exercise are stored. Groups should be mixed-ability: pair them higher–middle- and middle–lower-ability.

Hint

The only sentences in English that really need a passive verb are those where you don't know who has done the action, and then you can use 'someone', especially if you are speaking conversationally.

Lesson starter (15 minutes)

Discuss the difference between the passive and the active form of the verbs – see the Student Sheet.

Ask the students to look at the examples in English (Section 1). Which are active, which are passive?

Discuss the passive examples with them. How can they turn those into active sentences?

Main lesson (30 minutes)

Now get the students to look at the examples in French (Section 2). Explain that you use 'être' and the past participle of the verb. Remind them of the perfect tense.

Explain the use of 'on' in French, even when the passive is really needed. Complete the first couple of sentences with them (Section 3). Make sure they understand Section 4 – the passive as description – using past participles as adjectives.

Let them work through the examples in Sections 1–3 of the Student Sheet.

Plenary (10 minutes)

Check the answers to Sections 1–3 with the students.

Homework (5 minutes)

See the Student Sheet. Make sure that students understand what they have to do.

To make it harder

Ask the students to avoid using the same verbs as on the Student Sheet when they complete their homework.

To make it easier

Extend the plenary. Create ten sentences as directed for homework and record them on the whiteboard.

Make notes on this sheet. You need to know about the difference between passive and active verbs, but you will mainly use the active, which is what you have learnt up to now.

Section 1

Study these sentences in English. Which are active, which are passive?

1. I saw him yesterday.
2. He was eaten by a shark.
3. Papers were strewn all over the floor.
4. We shall eat the cakes.
5. They shall buy shoes.

6. The shoes will be bought by my father.
7. They will be paid for by my mother.
8. They've been eaten already.
9. A lad had been seen entering the room. We'll have to report him.

Section 2

1. La maison est construite.
2. La voiture est vendue maintenant.
3. Le magasin était fermé.
4. Le dîner est déjà terminé.
5. Des gâteaux seront offerts.

6. Les devoirs ont étés finis avant huit heures.
7. Les livres dans la bibliothèque ont été tous lus.
8. Les lettres sont laissées dans le vestibule.
9. La voiture a été lavée
10. Toute la limonade a été bue.

Section 3

Rewrite the sentences in Section 2 using 'on'.

Section 4

As your teacher has explained, these past participles are often used as adjectives – in both English and French. Try making up sentences with the following, making sure you are using the word as an adjective.

1. entouré
2. construit
3. fini
4. choisi
5. aimé

6. peint
7. nettoyé
8. connu
9. visité
10. vu

Homework

Write a passage in French, at least ten sentences long. Make one sentence passive, making sure that there is no way of avoiding it. Make one sentence using 'on'. Make one sentence using a past participle as an adjective.

Hint

You don't need to use this a lot, especially up to GCSE, but if you use it a little, with genuine understanding, you'll really impress.

❉ **Reminder: Have a go at a listening exercise.**

Verbs – Voice　　　　　　　　　　　　　　**STUDENT SHEET 57**

Aims and outcomes

To introduce students to the subjunctive and encourage them to use it.

Materials needed

- Student Sheet 58
- verb tables in dictionaries
- grammar books
- interactive whiteboard

Classroom setup

This is mainly a teacher-led activity though students may work in pairs on some of the exercises. They should be facing the teacher and the interactive whiteboard at all times.

Lesson starter (15 minutes)

Give an explanation of the difference between the subjunctive and the indicative. Explain some of the set times when the subjunctive is used and the general idea of it being for what is not real or certain. Point out that we have this mood in English, for example, in phrases like 'Long live the King!', 'May all your troubles be little ones!', 'If I were a rich man . . .'

Read through the list of indicators for the subjunctive.

Main lesson

(10 minutes)

Allow the students to work in pairs to interpret the sentences in the subjunctive and work out why they are in the subjunctive.

(10 minutes)

Explain the patterns and the irregular subjunctives. Encourage them to make up a few examples.

(10 minutes)

Students work in pairs to produce a few subjunctives.

Plenary (10 minutes)

Listen to the students' examples. Put a few on the whiteboard. Discuss the common ones on the sheet. Encourage the students to try to use at least one subjunctive in future pieces of written work. Point out that:

- they can often avoid it (see the Student Sheet)
- they can look these up, unless they are in an exam.

Homework (5 minutes)

Students should study the Student Sheet. They should learn a few examples of common subjunctive phrases off by heart – perhaps form the examples on the Student Sheet or from examples made up in class today.

To make it harder

Ask the students to find more examples of words that are always followed by the subjunctive.

To make it easier

Extend the plenary. Discuss with the students some subjunctive phrases that they have met today that will be useful. Record them on the whiteboard and ask students to note them down as items of vocabulary. They should learn these for homework.

FURTHER RESOURCES

The French Subjunctive *http://french.about.com/library/weekly/aa111599.htm*

When to use it *http://french.about.com/library/weekly/aa111799.htm*

The two moods

Verbs can be in two 'moods' in any language – indicative, which is what you have learnt already, and subjunctive, which we look at here and about which there is not quite so much to learn as about the indicative.

The subjunctive is essentially used for something that is not real.

Some examples of when you have to use the subjunctive

When you have to do something:

Il faut que

After some emotions:

Il est regrettable que   Il est surprenant que

When there is doubt or possibility:

Il est impossible que   Il est possible que   Il est improbable que

After the following words:

avant que	jusqu'à ce que	pourvu que	quoique
seul	unique	premier	dernier

When you know all these, check your resources to find more examples.

Some examples of verbs in the subjunctive

1. C'est la seule personne que je connaisse.
2. Il est regrettable qu'elle ne soit pas venue.
3. Il est impossible que je vienne.
4. Il faut qu'il le fasse.
5. Il est surprenant que le collège reste fermé.
6. Elle est contente quoiqu'elle aie beaucoup de devoirs.
7. Il est improbable qu'il sorte ce soir.
8. Pourvue qu'elle finesse ses devoirs elle peut regarder la télé.
9. Avant que je choisisse je dois les voir tous.
10. J'attends Jusqu'à ce qu'il arrive.

Note: Avant de partir, j'ai bu de l'eau – you can sometimes avoid it!

Formation

	parler	choisir	render
	parler	choisir	render
Stem	parl	choisiss	rend
Je (e)	parle	choisisse	rende
Tu (es)	parles	choisisses	rendes
Il (e)	parle	choisisse	rende
Nous (ions)	parlions	chosisssions	choisissions
Vous (iez)	pareliez	choisissiez	rendiez
Ils (ent)	parlent	chosissent	rendent

Some really useful ones:

Il faut je me'en aille

Il faut que je fassse

Il faut que je sache

Il est probable que je sois

✳ **Reminder: Have a go at a listening exercise.**

Aims and outcomes

To enable students to understand why word order is important and to show them how it works in French.

Materials needed

- Student Sheet 59
- verb tables in dictionaries
- grammar books
- interactive whiteboard

Classroom setup

This is mainly a teacher-led activity though students may work in pairs on some of the exercises. They should be facing the teacher and the interactive whiteboard at all times.

Lesson starter (15 minutes)

Make sure that the students understand effective and default word order which are referred to on the Student Sheet.

Discuss the examples with the students. You might touch on parts of speech here. This will be dealt with more thoroughly in a later grammar lesson.

Main lesson

(15 minutes)

Look at the first three questions with the students. Ask them to change the rest to the two alternative word orders. These are two examples of a mixture of effective and default word order.

(15 minutes)

Study 'Equipe de football' (the football team) with the students. This is now default word order.

Ask the students to make up some sentences in pairs.

Plenary (10 minutes)

Listen to some of the students' examples and write them on the whiteboard.

Homework (5 minutes)

Students should look at the question at the end and make up some more examples.

To make it harder

Ask the students to collect five more examples of each of the types of word order they have studied on the Student Sheet.

To make it easier

Extend the plenary. Make up some more examples with the students using the 'Equipe de football' from the Student Sheet and write these on the whiteboard. They may continue with these for homework if they find the last sentence on the Student Sheet difficult.

FURTHER RESOURCES

French word order *http://french.about.com/library/weekly/bltopicsub-wo.htm*.

Language Tutoring *www.languagetutoring.co.uk/WordOrder.html* is a useful article on French word order.

Effective and default word order

All languages have two sorts of word order:

Effective – where the word order makes a difference to meaning

Default – the normal word order, which you don't change unless changing it helps you to make your meaning clearer.

Effective word order

The good news about this is that French works in a very similar way to English. We use almost exactly the same word order to show who is doing what.

The person doing the action – the subject – comes first, then the verbs, then the person or thing that is having the action done to them – the object. Note: most adjectives come after their nouns.

Study the following sentences:

1. Je mange une pomme.
2. Il parle à son amie.
3. Elle a cassé la chaise.
4. Nous avons bu le vin.
5. Il a vu sa tante.
6. Vous avez réparé la voiture.
7. Elle veut acheter des gâteaux.
8. Elle va écrire une lettre.
9. Tu as choisi le pull vert.
10. Ils ont fini leurs devoirs.

Questions

1. Qu'est-ce que tu veux faire? Que veux-tu faire? Tu veux faire quoi?
2. Est-ce que tu as déjà choisi? As-tu déjà choisi? Tu as déjà choisi?
3. Quand est-ce qu'il arrive? Quand arrive-t-il? Il arrive quand?
4. Pourquoi est-ce qu'il veut quitter son emploi?
5. A quelle heure est-ce que les cours finissent?
6. As-tu un animal à la maison?
7. Est-il allé au ciné?
8. Que vas-tu faire demain?
9. Comment vas-tu en ville?
10. Quel journal lis-tu?

Equipe de football

Me						Je les leur donne.
Te	le					Elle me les offre.
	la	lui	y		en	Je leur en parle.
Nous	les	leur				Il y'en a cinq.
Vous						

Can you work out what is happening here? Je les ai mangés. Elle l'a vue. Ils les ont entendues.

❊ **Reminder: Have a go at a listening exercise.**

Aims and outcomes

To reinforce the students' knowledge and awareness of French prepositions.

Materials needed

- Student Sheet 60
- interactive whiteboard
- computers – at least one between two
- scissors and envelopes

Classroom setup

The first 15 minutes of the lesson should be a plenary with the students facing you and the interactive whiteboard. The students then work in pairs at the computer. The last 10 minutes of the lesson is also a plenary.

Hint

Make sure you keep copies of this work. Make sure the preposition game is an ongoing activity.

Lesson starter (15 minutes)

Make sure that the students understand each section of the Student Sheet. Explain the task described below.

Main lesson (30 minutes)

In pairs, the students invent games and exercises to help each other learn the prepositions. They should be given a warning after 20 minutes that they have just 10 minutes left and must 'make up' any game or exercise so that it can be used by another group. To ensure that there is variety, you may like to start off each pair on a different task.

Some suggestions:

- pairs using single prepositions
- pairs using sentences English/French
- flip the card (vocabulary learning – the answer is on the back)
- gap-filling
- quiz game
- create a description/set of instructions
- cards with half sentences on them
- verb and choice of three prepositions card game
- picture and true or false statements
- a new list of verbs and prepositions – *http://french.about.com/cs/grammar/a/verbswithprep.htm* gives you a useful list of verbs and their prepositions

Plenary (10 minutes)

Let each group present their games. Organize a grand swap.

Homework (5 minutes)

Students should complete somebody else's game for homework.

To make it harder

Ask the students to use *http://french.about.com/cs/grammar/a/verbswithprep.htm*

To make it easier

Extend the plenary and create an example of a game on the whiteboard with the students. Homework could then be to invent another game.

Prepositions tell us something about where something or somebody is in time or space – 'positions' – and occur in front of other words – 'pre'.

Good news

Most of them are very similar to those in English. For instance:

après	devant	selon
avant	derrière	sous
contre	entre	sur
dans	pour	

But watch out for

à côté de (du / de la / de l' des)

en face de

près de

And then some real oddities

chez depuis

Some things to watch out for

1. je joue au basket, au rugby, au foot aux échecques, etc.   je joue de la trompette, du piano

2. en France   au Japon   aux Etats-Unis

    Allemagne   au Canada

    Suisse   au Pays Bas

3. à pied   en voiture   par le train

    vélo   avion

    cheval   voiture

    pied   autobus

And oh, those verbs!

There are tons of them, and they're rarely the same as English. When you've learnt these, collect some more. Treat them as vocabulary.

s'approcher de	assister à	commencer à	compter sur
croire en	décider de	empêcher de	entrer dans
essayer de	faire attention à	finir par	hésiter à
s'intéresser à	manquer à	manquer de	se moquer de

✳ **Reminder: Try building some more haikus.**

Aims and outcomes

To make sure that students understand all the different components of a sentence in French and how to put them together.

Materials needed

- Student Sheet 61 – two copies each
- interactive whiteboard
- highlighter pens – one pack of yellow, pink, green and blue per table.

Classroom setup

Tables should be arranged for four students, but so that they can still see the interactive whiteboard. Groups should be mixed ability: pair them higher–middle and middle–lower abilty. Load sample sentences on the whiteboard.

Lesson starter (15 minutes)

Remind the students about how word order determines who does what in a sentence in French and is almost – but not quite – the same as English. Discuss the sample sentences on the whiteboard. Make sure the students understand finite verbs, subjects, direct objects, indirect objects, adjectives and adverbs.

Main lesson (30 minutes)

Students work in their groups and mark up the 'test' sentences as directed on the Student Sheet.

Plenary (10 minutes)

Correct student work with them. Give them all the correct answers and let them make a good copy on their second sheets. Make sure they understand the homework.

Answers (available also on the Continuum Companion website *http://education.james.continuumbooks.com*)

Verbs	jouent, ont, jette
Nouns	Marie, son frère, ballon are nouns. Ils/le/lui are pronouns.
Subjects	Marie et son frère, ils are subjects.
Objects	balloon, le,
Indirect objects	Luc, lui
Adjectives	petit, rouge, joli
Adverbs	heureusement
Adverbial phrase	dans le jardin

Homework (5 minutes)

As described on the Student Sheet.

To make it harder

Ask students to create their own example for each part of speech.

To make it easier

Provide students with a marked-up Student Sheet to take home.

Parts of Speech

You need some parts of speech, such as the subject, to build a sentence and you always need a finite verb otherwise a group of words is not a sentence.

Sample sentences

Marie et son petit frère jouent hereusement dans le joli jardin. Ils ont un ballon rouge. Marie jette le ballon à Luc. Elle lui le jette.

Finite verbs – These are the parts of the verb that 'work'. Sometimes there is more than one part. For example, in 'je suis allé' 'je' is the subject and 'suis allé' is the verb. Put a ring around each verb in the test sentences below.

Subject – This is a person or a thing. It may be a noun, or several nouns, or a pronoun. Underline each noun. Put a wavy line under each pronoun. Highlight the subjects in yellow.

Object – This is the person or thing to whom or to which the action is being done directly. Remember the pronouns: me, te, se, nous, vous le, la, les. Highlight in blue.

Indirect object – This is the person or the thing to whom or to which the action is being done indirectly. Remember the pronouns: me, te, se, lui, nous, vous, leur. Highlight indirect objects in green.

Adjectives – These describe words. They often come after the noun in French but not always. Put a box around all the adjectives.

Adverbs – These describe an action. Put a star by any adverbs.

Adverbial phrase – This is a phrase telling you where, why, when or how something happened.

Test sentences

J'habite une grande maison dans le nord de l'Angleterre. J'aime beaucoup ma maison. Mon père a acheté cette maison parce que ma grand-mère lui a donné £50,000 il y a cinq ans. Le jardin est assez grand. J'y joue avec mes frères après les cours. S'il fait chaud, ma mère nous donne des glaces. Parfois ma sœur arrive avec ses amies. Je n'aime pas ça. Elles parlent trop. Elles ne veulent jamais jouer au foot. La semaine prochaine, elles partiront en Allemagne. Nous aurons de la paix!

Hint

You don't need to remember the names of all the parts of speech, but you do have to remember they are the building blocks of language.

Homework

Make up ten sentences in French. Each one must have at least two other components. Make sure you use all of the components above at least once.

❄ Reminder: Practise extending and enhancing your personal oral questions.

Parts of Speech   **STUDENT SHEET 61**

Aims and outcomes

To make students aware of how much more visible gender and number are in French.

Materials needed

- Student Sheet 62
- grammar books and dictionaries
- interactive whiteboard

Classroom set up

Mixed-ability groups of four to six, mixed higher–middle- and middle–lower-ability. Make sure students can move easily from looking at the whiteboard to working in their groups.

Lesson starter

(15 minutes)

Explain that French can be funny. Discuss the first passage on the Student Sheet with the class, translating literally: 'She is in my school bag.' Make sure you point out that English seems equally funny to the French learning it – because we don't refer to inanimate objects as 'he' and 'she'. We have this strange word 'it'.

Then discuss the remainder of the Student Sheet, making sure students understand each section. Start them off on the exercises, with each group beginning on a different one. The higher-ability group should start on the later ones.

Main Lesson (30 minutes)

Students work through the exercises on the Student Sheet.

Plenary (10 minutes)

Correct the exercises with the students and write the answers on the whiteboard.

Homework (5 minutes)

This is explained on the Student Sheet. Make sure your students understand.

To make it harder

Ask students to create five further questions on each section that may be completed by their peers.

To make it easier

Discuss each exercise. Let the students try it. Correct it with them, writing answers on the whiteboard.

EXTRA RESOURCES

French gender and number *http://french.about.com/library/begin/bl_nouns2.htm*.

French agreement *http://french.about.com/library/weekly/bl-agreement.htm*.

Gender, number and agreement in French *www.classroom-resources.co.uk/acatalog/Online_Catalogue_Gender__Number_and_Agreement_in_French_541.html*.

Zap French *www.zapfrench.com/French-Lessons/Genre.htm* provides more examples.

Understanding French articles and how they indicate gender and number *www.dummies.com/how-to/content/understanding-french-articles-and-how-they-indicat.html*

You may use dictionaries, grammar books or textbooks for any of these exercises.

1. French is funny

Translate the following into English literally:

Où est mon stylo? Le voilà. Il est sous mon lit. Où est ma règle? La voilà. Elle est sur ma table. Où sont mes crayons? Les voilà. Ils sont sur ma chaise. Où est mon argent? Le voilà. Il est dans ma poche. Où est ma pizza? La voilà. Elle est sur mon assiette. Où sont mes livres? Les voilà. Ils sont dans la machine à laver. Où est mon cahier? Le voilà. Il est sur la télévision. Où est ma lettre? La voilà. Elle est dans le chien. Où sont mes parents? Les voilà. Ils sont dans le jardin.

2. The four words for 'the' in French

Le (m), la (f), les (plurals), l' (singular for all words beginning with a vowel or silent 'h'). What would you use with the words below?

église, garage, parents, lac, auberge, hôtel de ville, boulangerie, fille, garçon, enfants

3. The two words for 'a'

Un (m), une (f). Note that *des* means 'some'

Which would you use with the words below?

pain, croissants, glace, sandwich, abricot, pomme, verre d'eau, bouteille de limonade, livre

4. Some

Du (m), de la (f), des (plural), de l' (singular – all words beginning with a vowel).

Which would you use in front of the following?

chocolat, pain, herbe, fruits, bière, limonade, eau, fromage, beurre, bonbons, chou, clients

5. His/her/its

The same word is used for all three. Don't worry – the meaning is always clear. But you must take note of the word they go with. Son (masculine and feminine words beginning with a vowel), sa (feminine), ses (plural). Translate the following phrases into French:

his book, her exercise book, his pencils, her ruler, his sandwiches, her lemonade, its tyres

6. Similar

Mon, ma, mes — my; ce (m), cet (m) beginning with a vowel, ces (plural) – this/these. Use each of these words three times.

7. Detective work 1

Find out the words for 'our', 'your' (both sorts), and 'their' – masculine, feminine and plural. Any trouble with vowels?

8. Detective work 2

Adjectives also agree. Normally, you just add an 'e' for feminine and a 's' for plurals. But there are lots of exceptions. Search your grammar books for ten examples to share with your classmates. Now, see if you can find five nouns that have odd plurals.

9. Changes

Study the following passage and then write it out again according to the suggested changes.

Jaques s'est réveillé à sept heures. Il s'est levé. Il s'est douché. Il a pris le petit déjeuner. Il est parti à huit heures. Il a pris l'autobus. Il est arrivé à huit heures et quart.

Tell the same story about Jeanne, then Marc et Pierre, then Claudine et Marie, and finally about M et Mme Duclos.

10. Quiz

What do you know about the 'preceding direct object' for verbs that take 'avoir ' in the past?

Homework

Redo the 'mon, ma, mes' exercise and Detective work 2.

Hint

Carry on collecting odd adjectives and plurals.

Always check your written work for agreements.

❊ **Reminder: Revise parts of speech.**

Gender and Number

STUDENT SHEET 62

Aims and outcomes

Although strictly speaking we are talking about usage or vocabulary here, these three ingredients need to be at the tips of students' tongues and brains if they are to have mastery of their French. This lesson aims to introduce the student to ways to 'fix' this easy-to-understand but hard-to-remember subject matter.

Materials needed

- Student Sheet 63 – but do not give it out until the end of the lesson
- interactive whiteboard
- bingo game (you can often purchase small packs of bingo sheets in a booklet – a little like cloakroom tickets)
- lots of scrap paper

Classroom setup

Tables of four to six. There should, if possible, be even numbers at each table – students will be working in pairs during some parts of the lesson. Complete mixed-ability works for this.

Lesson starter (10 minutes)

Look at Student Sheet 63 with the class to:

Revise numbers up to 31 and dates. You could already have these loaded on the whiteboard and reveal as you discuss.

Revise numbers to 100, but also 1,000s.

Revise both types of time.

Main lesson (35 minutes)

Now play some games:

Birthday line-up. Students have to stand in a ring around the classroom and ask each other 'C'est quand ton anniversaire?' If their birthday is later in the year than the person they speak to, they move clockwise, if earlier, anti-clockwise. See how long it takes for them to get into order.

Play bingo with the whole class, then bingo in smaller groups, then number swap where pairs dictate four figure numbers – possibly years – to each other. They should write down five each, then dictate them to their partner. They check them afterwards. If there is a discrepancy, they have to see who made the mistake. They should do this as rapidly as possible.

Play pair dictations with both types of time, as they did for numbers.

Play 'Je suis allé(e) au marché et j'ai acheté . . .' Each person repeats the statement of the one before and adds an item.

Plenary (10 minutes)

Team quiz. Divide the group into two and test them on numbers, times and quantities.

Homework (5 minutes)

Students should thoroughly revise numbers, times and quantities.

To make it harder

In the quiz, fire large numbers at the students rapidly.

To make it easier

In the quiz and the games, allow students to work in pairs. In games that are already for pairs, allow the students to work in fours.

Understand and learn the following.

Numbers

un	douze	trente
deux	treize	quarante
trois	quatorze	cinquante
quatre	quinze	soixante
cinq	seize	soixante-dix
six	dix-sept	soixante-onze
sept	dix-huit	quatre-vingts
huit	dix-neuf	quatre-vingt-dix
neuf	vingt	cent
dix	vingt et un	cent trois
onze	vingt-deux	mille

Months

janvier, février, mars, avril, mai, juin, juillet, août, septembre, octobre, novembre, décembre, le premier mai, le trente juin

Times

une heure	cinq	une heure	cinq	le samedi
deux heures	dix	douze heures	dix	en mai
midi	et quart	treize heures	quinze	il y a . . . deux
minuit	vingt		vingt	semaines
	vingt-cinq		vingt-cinq	hier
	et demie		trente	demain
	moins vingt-cinq		trente-cinq	aujourd'hui
	moins vingt		quarante	en deux
	moins le quart		quarante-cinq	semaines
	moins dix		cinquante	pour/pendant
	moins cinq		cinquante-cinq	deux semaines

Quantities

une bouteille de	un kilo de	une livre de	cent grammes de	une boîte de
un paquet de	une portion de	une tranche de	une tasse de	un verre de

✳ **Reminder: Revise gender and number.**

Revision

Aims and outcomes

To get students to understand what they need to revise.

Materials needed

- Student Sheet 64
- students' own notes
- interactive whiteboard
- any other revision guides you have
- highlighters

Classroom setup

This is very much a teacher-led lesson for the first third, followed by a period where students work on their own. The final third is again teacher-led.

Lesson starter (15 minutes)

Discuss the mindmap on the Student Sheet. Make sure the students understand all the terms. Briefly discuss the importance of each one and decide with the students what will make the biggest difference in the exam for which they are studying.

Main lesson (30 minutes)

Let the students complete the Student Sheet on their own. They should highlight in one colour all the things they know really well. They should use a second colour for those areas they know less well. They should use a third colour for those areas they are worried about. They could use a fourth colour for anywhere they feel they know nothing at all.

Students should then list in order of importance all the areas they need to revise. The list should start where they know nothing, progressing through to those that they know less well. Within each category, they should list the items in order of what they feel is important.

Allow students some time also to study the revision guides you have available.

Plenary (10 minutes)

Discuss with students where their main strengths and weaknesses lie and whether it is better to use the revision guides available or to use their own notes, or a combination of both. If they choose the latter, then discuss what the balance should be.

Hint

There is no clear right or wrong answer to this. Often, a revision guide can feel overwhelming. They may present items in a different order from the way your students have learnt them, or may emphasize certain areas because they are geared towards a specific exam. Well-meaning parents can cause all sorts of trouble by buying a revision guide – this can cause confusion and unease.

Aim to identify a guide that will work effectively for your students – and then show them how to use it.

Homework (5 minutes)

Students should make a start on revising the area they have identified as their weakest.

To make it harder

Ask the students to extend the mindmap.

To make it easier

Ask the student to make two simple lists from the mindmap – one of what they know well and one of what they know they need to work some more on.

FURTHER RESOURCES

French Revision *www.frenchrevision.co.uk* provides a general introduction to revision.

Bite size *www.bbc.co.uk/schools/gcsebitesize/french* divides revision into bite size pieces.

Parsons, R. (2001) *GCSE French Revision Guide*. Cumbria: Coordination Group Publications.

Parson, R. (2003) GCSE French: Complete Revision and Practice. Cumbria: Coordination Group Publications.

Look at the mindmap. Highlight in one colour all those items you know really well. Use a second colour to identify what you know less well. Use a third colour for any items that you feel decidedly uncomfortable with and if you feel very uncomfortable with anything use a fourth colour. Now write a list of what you need to revise, starting with what you know least well. Your teacher will give you some help with this. Finish off your list for homework.

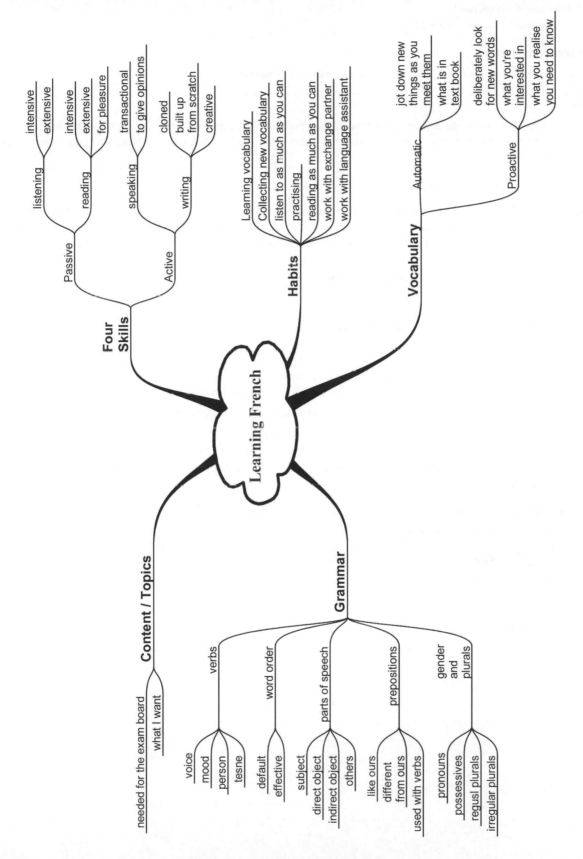

❊ Reminder: Take a look through some marked work and see if you can improve it.

Aims and outcomes

To aid students in planning their revision.

Materials needed

- Student Sheet 65
- interactive whiteboard
- sheets and lists from Lesson 64

Classroom setup

This is a teacher-led lesson with students working individually for some of the time.

Hint

A tip to pass on to students: as they work though their revision plan, they may find they get through some sections more quickly than they thought. That is because having learnt one area another, based on that, then goes a lot quicker than anticipated.

Lesson starter (15 minutes)

Explain the difference between active revision and passive revision. Passive revision might include looking through lists, corrected work, readings that have already been completed. Active revision might mean learning some things by heart and practising various skills, perhaps with their tandem partner. Also discuss with students which activities should be done with other people.

Make sure that students understand the Student Sheet.

Main lesson (30 minutes)

Students should fill in the Student Sheet with their list from Lesson 64.

Plenary (10 minutes)

Discuss some of the sheets that students have filled in. Show them how they can revise those items. Show them where they can get help. Get them to mark up activities that would particularly benefit from involving their tandem partner.

They now need to plan how much time they will devote to each part and when they will do each bit.

Introduce the idea of a critical time plan. This is all about working backwards from the end date, that is, starting with the exam as the 'goal' date. They should now write out their revision plan in an order that makes sense.

Also point out that each of them will probably have a better time of the day for active revision. Plan bouts of active and passive revision accordingly.

Homework (5 minutes)

Continue with the 'critical time plan'.

To make it harder

Ask the students also to plan what times of day may be best for what they have identified as active revision and as passive revision.

To make it easier

Work with the whole class throughout the lesson.

	Passive Revision	Active Revision
With others		
Alone		

❋ Reminders: Take a look at the big picture – what is involved in learning a language?

Aims and outcomes

To remind students of how they might revise for the French oral exam.

Materials needed

- Student Sheet 66
- interactive whiteboard (if possible, with the oral lesson still recorded)
- all the oral Student Sheets:10–22
- students' own notes
- notes and sheets from Lessons 64 and 65

Classroom setup

Students will need to face you, but will also need to work with a partner – perhaps their current 'oral partner' – the person with whom they have agreed to practise oral work.

Hint

There are so many possibilities here for working with a tandem partner. Make sure they are aware of these.

Lesson starter (15 minutes)

Explain the three components of the oral exam: role play, the presentation and the general questions.

Discuss the student booklet for the oral exam. Make sure that students understand Student Sheet 66.

Main lesson (30 minutes)

Allow students to look through Student Sheet 66 with their partner. They may try some of the activities suggested. The aim, with the help of their partner, is to identify a set of actions they should take to improve their oral work.

Plenary (10 minutes)

Discuss with students what they have found out. Discuss with them how they might further enhance their speaking work.

Ask students to create a plan for oral revision, based on the plans they have made already. Ensure they specify what they are going to do and when. If there is 'homework' time left, they can start on this action plan.

Homework (5 minutes)

Students should spend at least another hour on their oral practice.

To make it harder

Ask students to devise a selection of essential phrases and questions for someone going to live or work in a French-speaking country.

To make it easier

Instead of giving students all of the extra Student Sheets, put together a few examples from each.

Remember, there are three parts to the French oral exam: role play, presentation and general questions.

Revising the role play

Practice the given situations.

Adapt and extend your role plays.

Work your way through all those situations.

Work with your tandem partner: Practise and extend and adapt.

Active: Practise with your role play friend.

Passive: Look through role play and appropriate vocabulary lists.

The presentation

Practise your presentation out loud – to your friends, your family, even your cat.

Get someone – your tandem partner, the language assistant or your oral friend – to ask you extra questions.

Work with your tandem partner: get them to listen to your presentation and ask you extra questions. Ask them to make a similar presentation to you.

Active: Practise with whoever is willing to listen.

Passive: Look over your presentation. Listen to a recording of it.

Personal questions

Ask someone – your friend, the language assistant, or your tandem partner – to ask you the open-ended questions and any extension questions.

Run through the build-up questions as well.

Work with your tandem partner: get them to ask you questions and correct your mistakes. Ask your partner the same questions. Your partner answers your questions and extends on them.

Active: Work over the questions.

Passive: Read though your questions and answers. Listen to your recording.

✷ **Reminders: Do some revision for the listening exam.**

Aims and outcomes

To equip students with the knowledge of how to revise for the listening exam and give them some practice in it.

Materials needed

- Student Sheet 67
- some old listening papers – at least one Foundation and at least one Higher.
- listening posts

Classroom setup

Students should be grouped around tables of six. Have one activity on each table and spare activities at the front.

Hint

If you are not already doing so it would be a good idea now, as we approach the exam, to provide your student with plenty of opportunities for practising listening. For example, you could provide them as downloadable audio files from your school website (but be aware that normally the site licence that comes with your audio material does allow you to copy it for students).

Lesson starter (10 minutes)

Make sure students understand the Student Sheet.

Main lesson (35 minutes)

Organize the students so that different groups start with different activities. They should work through as many of the listening activities as they can in this time. They should also take time to discuss the Student Sheet.

Plenary (10 minutes)

Discuss the ideas about revision on the Student Sheet.

Homework (5 minutes)

Ask students to work individually on their 'listening revision plan'.

To make it harder

Use only Higher Listening papers and also provide some listening material aimed at native speakers of French.

To make it easier

Give the students some lists of vocabulary on areas in which you know they are weaker.

FURTHER RESOURCES

Higher Listening *www.gcse.com/french/listening_higher.htm*.

GCSE French revision *www.saltgrammar.org.uk/pdf/GCSEFrenchrevision.pdf* provides a list of links to resources for listening.

Revilo Resources *www.revilolang.com/revision.cfm* provides resources for listening.

Revising for the Listening Exam

You can use both active and passive revision for listening. Work through these with your group – your teacher will tell you where to start.

Types of revision

Here are some activities you might do to help develop listening skills. Decide with the rest of your group which are active and which are passive. Can you add any others?

- Look through topic-based lists of vocabulary
- Learn lists of vocabulary from your vocabulary book
- Have a go at old listening 'papers'
- Listen to a French music channel
- Get your tandem partner to send you some sound files
- Set your DVD to French
- Look out for French films on TV
- Listen to a French radio station
- Find free internet resources

Foundation listening

Have a go with your group. Work as a group, but go through the normal stages of listening. Try to 'collect' at least six items of vocabulary that are new to all of you – either what you have heard or what you have read on the exam paper.

Using your tandem partner

Work with your group on thinking of how you could ask your tandem partner to help you with listening activities. Try to get a good balance of active and passive activities.

Higher listening

Have a go with your group. Work as a group, but go through the normal stages of listening. Try to 'collect' at least six items of vocabulary that are new to all of you – either what you have heard or what you read on the exam paper.

Your listening revision plan

Work out how you are going to revise listening. How much active and how much passive are you going to use? Identify any topic areas where you need to revise. How will you use your tandem partner? Integrate this into your general revision plan. Also remember to timetable in a review opportunity.

✳ Reminders: What else do you still need to revise?

Aims and outcomes

To equip your students with the knowledge and skills to revise for the reading exam.

Materials needed

- Student Sheet 68
- interactive whiteboard
- examples of old reading papers
- other reading materials

Classroom setup

Students should work individually through this.

Hint

Consider having a bank of reading materials similar to what you have today that students can borrow either in hardcopy or download from a members-only part of a website.

Lesson starter (15 minutes)

Discuss 'Types of revision', 'Working with your tandem partner' and 'Strategies for continued improvement' from the Student Sheet.

Main lesson (30 minutes)

Allow students to work with the reading materials, trying out the strategies.

Plenary (10 minutes)

Discuss 'My revision plan' from the Student Sheet with students.

Homework (5 minutes)

Students should complete their revision plan according to the guidelines on the Student Sheet.

To make it harder

Ask students to add their own ideas for reading revision.

To make it easier

Ask students to select three reading revision activities they will try in the next two weeks.

FURTHER RESOURCES

GCSE Reading Revision *www.gcse.com/french/reading_higher.htm* provides Higher Reading resources.

You can use both active and passive revision for reading. Work through these with your group – your teacher will tell you where to start.

Types of revision

Here are some activities you might do for your reading revision. Decide with your teacher which are active and which are passive. Can you add any others?

- look through topic-based lists of vocabulary
- learn lists of vocabulary from your vocabulary book
- have a go at old reading papers
- look at a French online magazine
- look at common websites in French such as Amazon, Yahoo, Google
- look out for free French reading material when you are in a French-speaking country
- work your way through the reading materials your teacher provides

Working with your tandem partner

Your tandem partner can:

- send you emails
- send you reading material
- recommend books
- recommend websites
- find materials specific to topics you are studying
- write about specific topics that you are studying

Strategies for continued improvement

These activities may be useful:

- spend some time on extensive reading
- spend some time on intensive reading
- spend some time on going over reading you have done before
- when revising actively, always try to learn five new words
- work through the materials provided by your teacher – always go for something that is a little bit harder

My revision plan

Look at your list of active revision and passive revision.

Plan how much time you want/are able to spend on each, and when it is best for you to do each.

Within your active revision slots, plan how much time you want to spend on:

- extensive reading
- intensive reading
- extra reading
- vocabulary building

✳ Reminders: What do you still need to do for the oral exam? For role play? Presentation? Personal questions?

Aims and outcomes

To show students strategies for revising effectively for the writing exam.

Materials needed

- Student Sheet 69
- students' corrected work
- old exam papers
- pieces of writing that can be used for 'cloning'

Classroom setup

The lesson will be partly teacher-led. The students will work individually and in pairs.

Lesson starter (10 minutes)

Make sure students understand the Student Sheet.

Main lesson

(10 minutes)

Ask students to look through some work that has already been corrected. They must make sure they understand why every single mistake is a mistake.

(10 minutes)

Ask students to write a diary extract.

(10 minutes)

Get students to swap work with their partners and check the written work according to the instructions on their sheet.

Plenary (15 minutes)

Remind students that they will need to think about what they will do to maximize revision for the writing exam.

Give each student a handful of materials – texts they can clone, other examples of good writing, and old exam papers. Give them some choice. This is something they can work through over the next few days/weeks. Encourage them to take as many examples as possible.

Homework (5 minutes)

Ask them to make a revision plan for writing.

To make it harder

Ask students to hand in a copy of their plan. In two weeks' time arrange one-to-ones so that you can check how well they are completing their plan.

To make it easier

Ask students to identify three areas where they can improve their writing and what they will do about this over the next two weeks.

Types of revision

Consider the following:

- Looking through corrected work
- Asking another student to look over your work and your doing the same for them
- Keeping a simple diary in French and handing it in for correction every so often. Remember to check it yourself as well
- Getting your tandem friend to correct some of your work for you
- Getting your tandem friend to send you examples of good writing to memorize
- 'Cloning' some good written material
- Revising grammar
- Going through old exam papers

Note that these progress from more passive revision to more active revision.

Looking over corrected work

Make sure you understand why all the mistakes are mistakes. If you don't, ask you teacher. If she isn't available, ask another student or your tandem partner.

Working with other students

Find a writing friend. Do a piece of writing and get your writing friend to check your work for you. Your teacher may also be able to supply you with old exam papers or other pieces of writing you can try to clone.

Writing checklist

Check for one thing at a time:

- verbs – tense, voice, mood and person
- word order – default and effective
- prepositions – the same as ours, different, extra, with verbs
- gender and number
- your own peculiar mistakes (and revise any of these grammar points about which you are not sure of).

Diary writing

Try to write at least 100 words a day. Always have a mixture of tenses. Always get this work checked.

Your tandem friend

Your tandem friend checks your work and can give you examples of good writing. Ask them to write about specific topics that will help you.

Your revision plan

Slot some of these revision activities into you overall revision plan.

❋ Reminder: Do some revision for the reading exam.

Revising for the Writing Exam   **STUDENT SHEET 69**

The Exam

Aims and outcomes

To enable students to feel confident about the oral exam.

Materials needed

- Student Sheet 70
- old oral exams or stylized ones that look simpler than actual exam papers
- students' own notes

Classroom setup

Mixed-ability groups of four. Two will take the part of teacher and two will take the part of students. When not taking part, they will observe the group.

Lesson starter (5 minutes)

Discuss the Student Sheet. Make sure that students understand what they need to do.

Main lesson

(10 minutes)

The first 'candidate' prepares for an oral exam, using one of the past papers, while the first 'teacher' gets ready for the 'exams'.

(15 minutes)

The second 'candidate' prepares, while the first 'teacher' and 'candidate' do the oral exam.

(15 minutes)

The second 'candidate' and the second 'teacher' perform the exam.

Plenary (10 minutes)

The whole class comes together to discuss what they saw in the 'oral exams'.

Homework (5 minutes)

Students should arrange a time and place for the other two in their group to have a go at a mock oral exam.

To make it harder

Set up another after school session where everyone has another chance to complete a mock oral, this time with you or the language assistant.

To make it easier

Split the main lesson into three parts. Allow a different pair to perform the role play, the presentation and the general questions. Use groups you know will perform well if not perfectly. Discuss with the whole class aspects of their performance.

FURTHER RESOURCES

BBC Bitesize *www.bbc.co.uk/schools/gcsebitesize/french/examskills/3speakingconversationrev1.shtml* is a short article about preparing for the speaking exam.

Speaking Exam *www.gcse.com/french/speaking.htm* gives some detials about the speaking exam.

On the day

Preparation time

You will be given 15 minutes before the exam to prepare the role play. Don't panic if at first you find it difficult. Repeat again and again in your head. You can talk out loud – even if there is someone sitting with you.

Try to work out what sort of things your teacher might surprise you with for the extra, unrehearsed question.

Take a few deep breaths before you go into the room.

In the room

Your teacher will greet you politely. Be as friendly and as positive as you can in return. After all, you have worked hard for this exam. Now it is time to enjoy yourself a little and show off. It is fine to be nervous – it may even make you perform better.

As the exam progresses

First comes the role play. The trickiest part will be the unrehearsed question. Don't worry if you don't understand – ask the teacher to repeat it.

Pardon, je ne comprends pas. Vous pouvez répéter, s'il vous plaît?

Next, though this depends on your exam board, is your presentation. Don't worry if you go blank. Your teacher will prompt you to keep going.

You will also be asked questions at the end. Again, don't worry if you don't understand. Just calmly ask your teacher to repeat.

Finally come the personal questions. Your teacher will probably start off with the open-ended ones and only give you specific ones if you dry up. Don't worry, but try to keep talking and to speak more of the time than your teacher. You might occasionally ask them a question.

Aim to include as many different tenses of verbs as you can – and perhaps even voices, moods and persons. Try to show off your grammar!

In class today

The tests

Try to make this as near to the real thing as possible. Don't worry if you don't get the chance to be the student. You learn almost as much by being a 'teacher' or an observer.

Giving feedback

Point out:

1. What your classmates did well
2. What they did less well
3. How they might best improve

❄ Reminder: What do you still need to do for the reading exam?

Aims and outcomes

To boost students' confidence about the listening exam.

Materials needed

- Student Sheet 71
- one old Higher Listening exam

Classroom setup

The room should be set up as if for an exam. As this is for listening, make sure the room is acoustically sound and that there will be little intrusion from outside noises.

Lesson starter (10 minutes)

Make sure students understand the Student Sheet.

Main lesson (35 minutes)

Conduct the mock exam.

Plenary (10 minutes)

Give students the correct answers and discuss their experiences.

Homework (5 minutes)

Spend more time on listening revision – revisit Student Sheet 67.

To make it harder

Give the students another Higher Listening paper to complete at home.

To make it easier

After students have listened for the first time, discuss in English the gist of what they have heard.

FURTHER RESOURCES

BBC Bitesize *www.bbc.co.uk/schools/gcsebitesize/french/examskills/1listeningexamrev1.shtml* gives advice about preparing for the French listening exam.

GCSE.com *www.gcse.com/french/listening.htm* provides a brief discussion about the listenign exam.

Classroom Resources *www.classroom-resources.co.uk/acatalog/Online_Catalogue_AQA_French_GCSE_Interactive_Past_ Papers__Higher_Tier_1248.html* describes some interesting interactive resources.

Some things to remember

You have worked hard. Yes, listening does require a lot of concentration and if you lose concentration for even a split second you can miss something vital, unlike reading or writing and to some extent speaking, where you can backtrack.

But why should you worry? You've worked hard, haven't you? And you can concentrate, can't you?

Reading skills are also needed

There are some parts of the paper, but only a few, where you need to use your reading skills as well. Remember, for the French parts, reading three times is useful: and remember to take short notes, perhaps in pencil, on what you've understood.

Don't neglect your skill at reading in your own language. Read the questions and task instructions carefully. Look at the number of marks awarded for each question and be aware that you need to make that number of points in your answer.

Listening carefully

Each exam has its own routines. Some boards/levels don't let you look at the questions first, some do. Even if they do, though, on the first hearing, you should generally be getting the main gist of the text. The second time round you can look at the questions.

There will be gaps in the audio file, bigger in the second and subsequent listenings. This gives you time to fill in the answers. If you don't finish, don't worry, a little time is allowed at the end. Leave this question and carry on listening.

The rule of three listenings

In some exams, although not generally in GCSE, you are allowed control of the sound file and can listen as many times as you like within a certain restricted time frame. Bear in mind, however, that in the short-term you might not understand any more after three listenings. There's an implication here for how you might do some revision.

Even in the short-term, though, your brain works away at decoding way beyond what your conscious mind can do. It's a miracle – so let it happen.

Don't leave any blanks

Take a shrewd look at those marks again. Give as many details as there are marks. If you think you've heard more detail, put them down anyway. Just avoid hedging bets. For example, you may have heard that Little Red Riding Hood was wearing a red cape made by her mother. The exam asks for two details. Although there are in theory three details, the story is so well known that 'red cape' may count as one answer.

Don't give contradictory answers. For example, don't say that the wolf was killed by both the woodcutter and Little Red Riding Hood's father – especially if you only get one point for the answer.

✳ **Reminder: What do you still need to do for the writing exam?**

Aims and outcomes

To boost students' confidence about the reading exam.

Materials needed

- Student Sheet 72
- one old Higher Reading exam

Classroom setup

The room should be set up as for an exam.

Lesson starter (10 minutes)

Make sure that students understand the Student Sheet.

Main lesson (35 minutes)

Conduct the mock exam.

Plenary (10 minutes)

Give students the answers and discuss their experience.

Homework (5 minutes)

Carry on revising for the reading exam. Revisit Student Sheet 68.

To make it harder

Provide the students with another Higher Reading paper to complete at home.

To make it easier

Discuss the gist of what they have read after the first ten minutes of the main lesson.

FURTHER RESOURCES

BBC Bitesize *www.bbc.co.uk/schools/gcsebitesize/french/examskills/2readingexamrev1.shtml* provides tips about reading exam.

GCSE.com *www.gcse.com/french/reading.htm* gives breif detials about the reaing exam.

Some things to remember

You have worked hard. You've learnt lots of vocabulary. You've had lots of reading practice. You've constantly tried to Improve. Now is the chance for you to show off what you can do.

The rule of three readings

Remember to read your text and your questions three times.

Bear in mind, however, that in the short-term you might not understand any more after three readings. There's an implication there for how you might do some revision.

Even in the short-term, though, your brain works away at decoding way beyond what your conscious mind can do. It's a miracle – so let it happen.

1. On the first reading, pencil in on your text a translation of everything you already know.

2. On the second reading, add in all words that remind you of English.

3. On the third reading, pencil in anything else that is obvious.

Do this also for the questions in French. Study the questions in English carefully.

Don't leave any blanks

Take a shrewd look at those marks again. Give as many details as there are marks. If you think you've heard more detail, put them down anyway. Just avoid hedging bets. For example, you may have read that the Sleeping Beauty is to prick her finger on a spinning wheel and die. The exam asks for one detail. Although there are in theory two here, the story is so well known that the whole incident may count as one.

Don't give contradictory answers: don't say Sleeping Beauty died when she only slept – especially if you only get one point for the answer.

✳ **Reminder: Revise for the writing exam.**

Aims and outcomes

To enable students to feel more confident about the writing exam.

Materials needed

- Student Sheet 73
- two old Higher Writing papers

Classroom setup

Exam conditions.

Lesson starter (15 minutes)

Make sure that students understand the Student Sheet. Discuss the first Higher Writing paper – establish tasks and start writing together.

Main lesson (30 minutes)

Complete the second Higher Writing paper in exam conditions.

This piece of writing should be taken in, marked and returned to the students as soon as possible.

Plenary (10 minutes)

Discuss what students found difficult and ask whether they have noticed any new strengths and weaknesses. Discuss how they might address any weaknesses.

Homework (5 minutes)

Students should carry on with their writing revision.

To make it harder

Ask the students to self-critique, then peer-critique before they give in the work.

To make it easier

Discuss the writing questions with the students before they start.

FURTHER RESOURCES

GCSCE.com *www.gcse.com/french/writing.htm* gives a few tips about the writing exam.

BBC Bitesize *www.bbc.co.uk/schools/gcsebitesize/french/examskills/6writingexamrev1.shtml* is a useful article about the writing exam.

BBC Bitesize – Checking your writing *www.bbc.co.uk/schools/gcsebitesize/french/examskills/9checkingyourwritingrev1.shtml* discusses checking written work.

How you gain marks in the exam

You gain marks in two main ways:

1. By providing the main content of what you are being asked to provide. You can get a good mark for this aspect of the exam even if your French is not perfect, as long as a friendly native speaker of French can understand you.

2. By writing in very good French.

Note that no matter how good your French may be, you cannot get high marks if you have not provided all the content. If you've provided only 75 per cent of the content, you can only get 75 per cent of the quality marks. They are, of course, the harder marks to get.

First things first

Spend at least five minutes studying the questions. Even make notes, as you might in an English Language exam. Look at how the marks are awarded. Try to make the detail you include match the number of marks.

What you write

You may know some chunks of French very well. This may be material you have used for your oral. Can you use it as it is? Can you adapt and 'clone' it to fit these exam questions? You may be able to produce some of the content this way. You will also need to rely on the vocabulary and grammar you know to build up language from scratch.

Try to include a good mixture of tenses and perhaps a couple of subjunctives and a justifiable passive. Show off your knowledge of how to construct sentences. Make sure you use a good amount of pronouns. Make sure you demonstrate that you know all about agreements. Show off your prepositions. Try to include some of those fascinating words you have collected.

Checking your work

Make sure you leave enough time for this. You should allow between a third and a quarter of the time available. Remember your checklist:

- make sure you have completed the task
- verbs (voice, person, tense, mood)
- word order (default and effective)
- prepositions (like English, different from English, after verbs)
- number and gender
- time and quantities
- your own favourite mistakes

�֎ **Reminder: Look at what you need to do in the oral exam.**

Diagnostic Sheets

Aims and outcomes

To enable students to become aware of how much vocabulary they know and what they can do to improve their knowledge.

Materials needed

- Student Sheet 74
- textbooks
- students' own exercise books and vocabulary books
- interactive whiteboard

Classroom setup

Groups of three to five. For this exercise, you can allow students to work in friendship groups.

Lesson starter (15 minutes)

Make sure students understand the Student Sheet. Allow the students to work through the first part of it individually.

Main Lesson (30 minutes)

Find out the most common areas that need revision. Allot each group of students a few areas to research. They should record their findings on paper or straight onto a computer document.

Plenary (10 minutes)

Allow each group to present their findings. If there is not time to complete all of them, collect in any extra sheets. Consider emailing results to students.

Homework (5 minutes)

Students should revise one of the areas they have highlighted today.

To make it harder

Students should identify and add other areas for revision.

To make it easier

Students may be asked to identify the five areas where they need to work the hardest and concentrate on those for the moment.

FURTHER RESOURCES

Learn French *www.lingolex.com/french.htm* and

About French *http://french.about.com/od/vocabulary/French_Vocabulary_Lessons_Lists.htm* provide some useful lists of vocabulary.

Freeway *www.happychild.org.uk/freeway/french/index.htm* provides topic based lists of vocabulary.

How much do you know?

Work through each of the areas listed below. Decide how much you know and award points: a lot (1), a fair amount (2), not much (3) or hardly any (4). Within your group, work first on the areas that score the least.

Home	Descriptions	Time
Family	Hobbies	Nature
School	Sport	Health
Holidays	Food	Town
Shops	Clothing	Public transport
Entertainment	Pets	Adjectives
Geography	Problems	Paragraph joining words
Future career	Colours	

Vocabulary gathering

In today's lesson you can gather vocabulary from the many resources here in the classroom. Your teacher also has a list of some online resources. Don't actually make lists of words today, but find out where you can find more vocabulary.

Spend about ten minutes on each area, starting with the highest scoring areas first. Try to break it down. For example, 'home' can be divided into 'rooms', 'garden', 'who does what where', 'my room', etc.

What you should do next

You need to carry on working on the areas you know less well. Remember the strategies you learnt about acquiring and learning vocabulary:

- collecting words as you go along
- dictionary work
- working with your tandem partner
- the wide-eyed walk

Look at those areas you know less well. Use all the resources pointed out to you today and use the strategies listed above to work on those areas. The difference at this point from what you have been doing up to now is that you now need to work a little more quickly to cover all the gaps.

✳ Reminder: Have another go at writing with the senses. What do you see, hear, smell, taste, feel?

Aims and outcomes

To enable students to be clear about which aspects of French grammar they need to spend more time on.

Materials needed

- Student Sheet 75
- grammar books and books with grammar in them
- some recently corrected work – preferably where the teacher has only pointed out the types of grammatical mistakes the student has made and has not actually corrected them
- the language assistant and other teaching assistants

Classroom setup

Students should work in pairs. Friendship groups or friend groups may work well, as long as ability is either matched, or mixed: middle–lower, or middle–higher. If all are the same ability, you may need to spend considerable time with lower-ability students.

Lesson starter (10 minutes)

Make sure students understand the Student Sheet.

Main lesson (35 minutes)

Students work through the diagnostic exercises. You and your helpers need to go around marking the work as students complete it. If you find some commonly occurring errors, you could pause the lesson and discuss these points by making notes on the whiteboard.

Students may help each other understand why their mistakes are mistakes and how they might correct them.

Plenary (10 minutes)

Discuss the outcomes of the exercises. Ask the students where they see the main problems and discuss how these might be addressed.

Homework (5 minutes)

Students plan how they are going to broaden their knowledge of French grammar.

To make it harder

Ask students to create another set of questions like the ones on the Student Sheet for their peers.

To make it easier

Complete each section with the students during the main part of the lesson. Explain each grammar concept again, allow them to complete the exercise, then correct the exercise with them.

FURTHER RESOURCES

About French *http://french.about.com/od/grammar/French_Grammar.htm* provides several useful articles about French grammar.

French Grammar Guide *www.languageguide.org/francais/grammar* provides some useful explanations about some aspects of French grammar.

French Grammar Tips and Articles *www.french-linguistics.co.uk/grammar* deals with some specific grammar problems encountered by English learners of French.

With your partner, work your way through this sheet in your rough book. Your teachers will mark your work. The number of answers you get right will determine how much your need to study any particular grammar point.

Verbs – tenses

Name all the tenses you can think of and give an example of a verb in each one.

Five or more correct answers, you're doing fine. You just need to polish up a little.

Verbs – person

Write sentences, with a different verb in each, using these pronouns:

Je ils elles tu il elle vous nous

Six or more right, you're doing fine.

Verbs–mood

Write two sentences in the indicative. Write two in the subjunctive. Say what they mean. What do we normally use the subjunctive for?

Four or more correct answers, you're doing fine.

Verbs–voice

Write two sentences in the active and two sentences in the unavoidable passive. Say what they mean. Write one sentence to show how you can use 'on' to avoid the passive. Say what it means.

Five or more correct, you're doing fine.

Word order

Write two sentences with normal word order and two where you've had to change it round. Say what they mean.

Put these words into the right order. Je les donne en lui. Say what it means.

Five or more correct, you're doing fine.

Prepositions

Give six prepositions, at least one of which we do not have in English, and say what they mean. Write two sentences containing verbs followed by prepositions. Say what they mean.

12 or more correct, you're doing fine.

Agreements

Give six words that have to agree. Give feminine, masculine, feminine plural and masculine plural.

20 or more right, you're doing fine.

Numbers, quantities and times

Write out the following numbers: 5, 17, 39, 67, 179, 1,289. Give four time expressions. Give four examples of clock time and four of 24-hour time.

15 or more right, you're doing fine.

✳ **Reminder: Have another look at grammar.**

Aims and outcomes

To enable students to get a sense of where they are at with listening and work out what they might do to improve.

Materials needed

- Student Sheet 76
- old Foundation and old Higher Listening paper from the same year

Classroom setup

Exam conditions. The room must be acoustically sound. The part of the lesson in which the students tackle the old paper will be conducted as an exam. We shall do half Old Foundation and half Old Higher Listening, including the 'crossover' sessions. You might want to merge the student questions sheet from the old exam papers so that it seems like a coherent document.

The rest of it will be a teacher-led plenary.

Lesson starter (10 minutes)

Explain that the class is going to complete half of a Foundation and half of a Higher Listening exam.

Remind them about the strategies for listening, about exam conditions and about the particular requirements of this exam board.

Main Lesson (30 minutes)

Conduct the listening paper.

Plenary (15 minutes)

Give out answers and the Student Sheet. Make sure that students understand the Student Sheet.

Homework (5 minutes)

Students devise an action plan as to how they are going to improve their listening, guided by the suggestions on the Student Sheet.

To make it harder

Ask students to write down the action they are taking as a result of this lesson. Check with them in two weeks' time that this has been completed.

To make it easier

Extend the plenary. Discuss some of the outcomes in more detail with the students.

FURTHER RESOURCES

BBC Bitesize *www.bbc.co.uk/schools/gcsebitesize/french/examskills/1listeningexamrev1.shtml* provides tips on how to prepare for the French listening exam.

French on the net *http://anne_fox.homestead.com/Bestlinks.html* provides a list of links to other good websites for French revision.

Listening

You are about to do a French listening practice exam. After you have finished it and the teacher has given you the answers, work your way through these questions.

Overall impression

Did the exam seem hard or easy or just about right? Did you get over 75 per cent of the available marks?

Let's aim high. If you found this exam hard or just about right, and you got less than 75 per cent there's probably lots of room for improvement. Read on to find out what you can do.

If you did get over 75 per cent, well done – but you can still improve. It's probably time to start listening to things French-speaking people listen to. So seek out French radio stations and TV stations. Set your DVDs to French.

Trouble understanding the questions?

This may have more to do with your reading skills. Revisit your reading advice sheets. Work on building up your vocabulary.

Trouble understanding the audio file?

This implies that you need more general listening practice. Combine 'real' listening with doing further practice papers. 'Real' listening includes listening to the radio, watching TV and listening to audio files your tandem partner sends you. Just listen to those items and don't worry too much about understanding everything. Let the language wash over you.

Your teacher may well have set up a bank of listening materials that you can access at school or at home via the school website. Work your way steadily through these. Try to start at about this level or perhaps a little lower. If working with easier material, make sure you understand every single word. Add any new items to your collected vocabulary. When working with harder materials, check your answers afterwards, and try to work out why you have got answers wrong.

Work on building up your vocabulary.

File and questions understood quite well, but marks still disappointing

This may be an exam technique problem. Always make sure you have as many details written down as there are marks for each question. Working through the practice papers will help with this. The reading exam papers will also help you, as will building up vocabulary.

Now make your plan

Work out a plan for the next week to improve your listening. Review the plan after a week.

❈ Reminder: Work out what you still need to do to improve your vocabulary to help with listening and reading.

Aims and outcomes

To make students more conscious of their own strengths and weaknesses when speaking.

Materials needed

- Student Sheet 77
- Students Sheets 10–22 for work to do with speaking
- the language assistant, if possible

Classroom setup

Students should work in fours. If students are still in 'oral friend' pairs, pair two groups together, perhaps mixing ability low and medium and medium and high.

Hint

There is a strong possibility that not everyone will get their turn on every section. Students should start with a different person for each section. They can of course carry on this work outside of the classroom.

Lesson starter (10 minutes)

Make sure students understand the Student Sheet.

Main lesson (35 minutes)

Students complete the exercises on 'Role play practice', 'Presentation practice', 'Personal questions' and 'Fluency, pronunciation and intonation' part of the sheet.

Plenary (10 minutes)

Discuss the outcomes of the exercises with the students.

Homework (5 minutes)

Individually, students write their action plans.

To make it harder

Ask the students to extend the number of situations in the Role Play and Personal Questions sections of the Student Sheet.

To make it easier

As you know your students, identify quickly for each one an area within the Role Play and Personal Questions on which they should work. This time the area should be one in which they are reasonably competent.

FURTHER RESOURCES

About French.com *http://french.about.com/library/pronunciation/bl-pronunciation.htm* provides pronunciation practice.

French audio dictionary *http://french.about.com/library/pronunciation/bl-audiodico.htm* provides audio files to aid pronunciation practice.

BBC *www.bbc.co.uk/languages/french/lj/pronunciation* provides some notes on French pronunciation.

This sheet gives you some exercises to do within your groups to help you determine how to shape your work on speaking over the next week or so. You might not complete each section within a lesson, so take it in turns being first. Consider carrying on with this after the lesson.

Role play practice

Work through the following situations. Two of you should perform a role play on one of the areas and the others should give you a mark out of ten for how well you do. As you listen, consider whether the 'performers' are using a good range of vocabulary. Do they sound as if they mean what they say? Do they sound natural, as if they understand each other well?

- shopping
- problems
- in a restaurant
- at school
- talking to your French-speaking exchange family

- public transport
- holidays
- free time and entertainment
- directions
- tourist office

You now need to revise the areas where you did less well.

Presentation practice

Take it in turns performing your presentation to the other students in your group. The other members of the group should ask questions. Mark each performer out of ten and give them feedback on the following:

- was it interesting?
- did they speak fluently and clearly?
- were they able to answer questions well?
- was there a variety of language, including different tenses in the verbs?

Now, work to improve the areas you did less well in.

Personal questions

Speak about the following:

- ta maison
- ta famille
- ton collège

- tes vacances
- tes amis
- tes passe-temps

Give each other marks out of ten.

How well do they answer questions?

How well do they answer the supplementary questions?

How fluently and clearly do they speak?

Do they include a variety of language, including different tenses in their verbs?

Fluency, pronunciation and intonation

Give marks for this.

Make out your action plan for the next week. Review it at the end. Remember listening will always help with speaking. Get your tandem partner to help.

✳ **Reminder: Revise for the listening exam.**

Aims and outcomes

To enable students to pinpoint their own strengths and weaknesses in reading and work out how to get on to the next stage.

Materials needed

- Student Sheet 78
- a variety of reading materials

Classroom setup

Students work completely individually in this lesson. It is almost like a private study period.

Lesson starter (10 minutes)

Make sure that students understand the Student Sheet. Ask them to start with a piece of reading that is one level above where they feel comfortable. Advise them that when they go on to the next piece of reading they might like to go to the level below where they feel comfortable.

Main lesson (35 minutes)

Students work through as many reading materials as they can in the lesson, using the guidelines on the Student Sheet.

Plenary (10 minutes)

Discuss strategies to help students go from one level to another.

Homework (5 minutes)

Students should take home another piece of reading, and make and start following an action plan to get them up to the next level.

To make it harder

Ask the students to work at two levels above where they feel comfortable for some of the time.

To make it easier

As you know your students, give them each their first piece of reading material. It should stretch them a little but not too much.

FURTHER RESOURCES

Globe Gate *http://globegate.utm.edu/french/globegate_mirror/reading.html* provides tips on how to make the most of reading in another language.

Lectures de France *http://lecturesdefrance.com/shop/index.php?action=item&id=2211* reviews authentic French reading materials for young learners, providing a fresh selection each week.

Revilo *www.revilolang.com/schools_cards.cfm* describes a reading resource which comes as a set of cards.

Assess where you are on this list. Consider what you need to do if you move up (towards the top of the page). Consider what you need to do if you move down (towards the bottom of the page).

- Books written for French-speaking people your age
- Magazines written for French-speaking people your age
- Brochures and pamphlets without many pictures
- Websites
- Brochures and pamphlets with lots of pictures
- Books and magazines written for French-speaking people who can't read very well
- Books and magazines written for people learning French

If you are moving down a level, you can probably treat the new level as intensive reading and be prepared to understand every single word. Look up every word you do not understand and learn these proactively as vocabulary.

To move up a level you need to be prepared to understand a little less but read more and more quickly.

Reading questions in the Listening and Reading exams is a form of intensive reading. Programme some time for practising this.

Try working at three levels for the next week: your natural level, at which you feel comfortable; the level above, which can stretch you a little; and the level below, which you now use as intensive reading and vocabulary building.

✳ Reminder: **Make a list of all the areas you need to revise.**

Aims and outcomes

To enable students to find out where they are at with writing and plan ways of improving.

Materials needed

- Student Sheet 79
- the language assistant, if possible

Classroom setup

Students should work individually.

Lesson starter (10 minutes)

Make sure students understand the Student Sheet.

Main lesson (35 minutes)

Students complete Task 1 on the Student Sheet.

As the students work, go around marking and commenting on their work. The language assistant should help. Try to shape your comments to the suggestions on the Student Sheet.

Once students have finished Task 1, they should read the suggestions on the sheet and decide on a different way of working. They should then try this out on Task 2.

Plenary (10 minutes)

Discuss any common mistakes you observed. Discuss with the class any particular difficulties they had. Also celebrate any successes.

Homework (5 minutes)

It is highly unlikely that students will finish all this work in the lesson, especially if you have interrupted them to discuss their work. You certainly won't have time to mark all their work with them unless you have a very small class. Make this an ongoing exercise – starting with homework tonight.

To make it harder

Give your students a real reason for writing – perhaps something to do with your tandem school.

To make it easier

Spend some time with weaker students kick-starting each exercise for them.

FURTHER RESOURCES

GCSE French Writing Tips *www.gcse.com/french/writing_tips.htm* provides simple tips on writing.

About French Writing *http://french.about.com/od/writing/French_Writing_Links_and_Resources_Write_in_French.htm* provides tips on writing at five different levels.

Today you are going to do some written tasks. In Task 1, you are asked to work as you normally would and try to observe what you are doing at the same time. In Task 2, you are asked to try something else. By the end of the exercise you should be really enjoying writing and showing off what you know. Your teacher will be doing her best to mark your work with you in class.

Below each task you will find some ideas about what else you might do, according to the marks you received.

Task 1

Write 150 words about 'Qu'est-ce que tu as fait pendant les grandes vacances l'année dernière?'

How easy do you find this?

Analysis: You write from what you know in your head but you can't say all that you really want to say.

Advice: Learn more by heart, but also try to use 'cloning' more often and think about building your own language by using grammar.

Analysis: You can easily adapt what you already know.

Advice: This is good. You get even more freedom if you can use grammar to build language.

Analysis: You are using grammar to build up language, but you are still a little limited and can't say everything you want to say.

Advice: You're on the right track. Just keep at it. Get your tandem partner to help you. Also, try to increase your vocabulary.

Analysis: You write naturally from what is in your head. You can say virtually everything that you want to.

Advice: Great. But don't stop working at it. You can very easily slip again. Consider keeping up the diary-writing.

After your work has been marked

Analysis: You have a low mark and have made lots of grammatical mistakes.

Advice: You need to build up your content more, practise the skills again and revise your grammar. Revisit Student Sheets 51–63. Don't despair. Make sure you know why your work is wrong and try to avoid those mistakes in the future.

Analysis: You don't have all that many grammatical mistakes but your mark is still low.

Advice: Make sure you have covered all the content and that your language is not too simplistic.

Analysis: Your mark is fine and there is not all that much comment from your teacher but still not 100 per cent.

Advice: Really try to show off with your content and your grammar.

Task 2

Write 150 words about 'Qu'est-ce que tu aimes faire le week-end?'

✳ Reminder: Do some extensive reading – read for information. You could use some internet resources.

Aims and outcomes

To encourage students to reassess where they are with their own language learning.

Materials needed

- Student Sheet 80
- a few copies of other sheets from this course
- textbooks, grammar books, reading and listening materials easily accessible
- as much of students' own work as they can carry to this lesson
- highlighter pens – three colours
- interactive whiteboard

Classroom setup

Groups of four to six. If at all possible, group them so that they share strengths and weaknesses.

Lesson starter (10 minutes)

Make sure students understand the mindmap on the Student Sheet.

Main Lesson

(10 minutes)

Students study the mindmap individually. They highlight in one colour areas they are confident in, they use another colour for areas in which they are less confident and they use the third colour for areas in which they know they have a lot of work to do.

(25 minutes)

Students work as a group on deciding what strategies to adopt for improving in the areas where most difficulties lie. They can access any materials in the room or their own folders for this. They should appoint a scribe and spokesperson for the group.

Plenary (10 minutes)

Groups give feedback on what they have found out. If you have a large class, you might not get round everyone. You could ask the first group to give information about the most common problem. The second group can also discuss the most common problem that they found. Other groups can add further comments about that problem. As you work through the groups, each one discussing only one problem, students should pick a problem that has not been discussed.

Even so, you might not cover everyone.

With a smaller group, however, you may run out of ideas: see the Hint below.

Students should be encouraged to take their own notes as you work through the 'problems'.

Hint

To avoid having too much or too little work, continue this activity for a few days after the lesson via a blog or a wiki.

Homework (5 minutes)

An absolutely free choice today. Point out to your students that by now they have so many good habits and know so much about how they learn that they can decide for themselves how they should best spend their allotted time before the next time they see you.

To make it harder

Ask students to extend the mindmap.

To make it easier

Ask students to identify just five areas in which they would like to improve.

Study the mindmap. Highlight each area according to how well you work in this area. Use one colour for what you're completely happy with, a second colour for what needs a little more work and a third colour for areas that need a lot of work.

You will then work with the other students in your group to decide on what you can do to improve in that area.

You will be asked to give feedback to the rest of the class, so your group needs a spokesperson and a scribe. You may be invited to join a blog or wiki forum after the lesson.

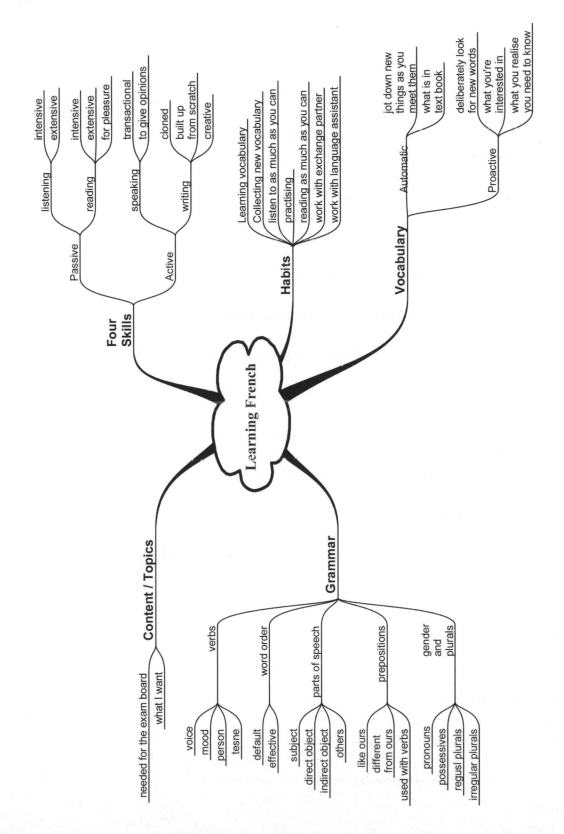

✳ Reminder: Revise your presentation for your oral. Go back to basics and see if there is anything you can improve.

Reading List

General resources

Authentik On Line, 2009.

Authentik Interactive is Here: www.authentikinteractive.com

BBC, 2009.

Better Languages: www.bbc.co.uk/languages/better

BBC Bitesize, 2009.

French Topics: www.bbc.co.uk/schools/gcsebitesize/french

Bonjour de France, 2009.

Cours de Français en France: www.bonjourdefrance.com/index/indexapp.htm

Bubl Link, 2009.

French Language: http://frenchinaclick.com/frenchinaclick2008/topics.shtml

Buxton Online, 2009.

Learn French Online: www.realfrench.net/index.php

Fox, Anne, 2009.

French on the Net: http://anne_fox.homestead.com/Bestlinks.html

Happy Child, 2009.

French: www.happychild.org.uk/freeway/french/index.htm

Lingolex, 2009.

Learn French: www.lingolex.com/french.htm

Multilingual Books, 2009.

Free French Lessons and Courses: http://multilingualbooks.com/freelessons-french.html

Real French, 2009.

Home: www.realfrench.net/index.php

SBS Langs, 2009.

French Resources: www.sbslangs.org.uk/frlinks.htm

Seven Kings High School, 2009.

GCSE French: www.sevenkingsmfl.typepad.com

General Revision

French Revision, 2009.

Home: www.frenchrevision.co.uk

Salt Grammar, 2009.

French Revision: www.saltgrammar.org.uk/pdf/GCSEFrenchrevision.pdf

Grammar

About.com.

Accord French Agreement: http://french.about.com/library/weekly/bl-agreement.htm

Asking Questions in French: http://french.about.com/library/weekly/aa022600t.htm

Beginning French: www.french-linguistics.co.uk/grammar

French Grammar: www.french-linguistics.co.uk/grammar

French Grammar: http://french.about.com/od/grammar/French_Grammar.htm

French Subjunctive: http://french.about.com/library/weekly/aa111599.htm and *: http://french.about.com/library/weekly/aa111799.htm*

Making French Nouns Feminine and Plural: http://french.about.com/od/grammar/a/nouns_3.htm

Word Order: http://french.about.com/od/wordorder/Word_Order.htm

Verbs with Prepositions: ttp://french.about.com/cs/grammar/a/verbswithprep.htm

Classroom Resources

Gender, Number and Agreement in French: http://french.about.com/library/weekly/bl-agreement.htm

French Linguistics

www.french-linguistics.co.uk/grammar

How to Ask Questions in French: www.french-linguistics.co.uk/grammar/questions.shtml

French and France

How to Ask Questions in French: http://en.wordpress.com/tag/how-to-ask-questions-in-french

French Beginner

How to Ask Questions in French: http://france-say.blogspot.com/2008/08/how-to-ask-questions-in-french.html

Indo-European Languages

French Tutorials Index: www.ielanguages.com/french.html

Language Guide

French Grammar: www.languageguide.org/francais/grammar

Language Tutoring

Word Order: http://french.about.com/od/wordorder/Word_Order.htm

Learn French

Asking Yes-No Questions in French: www.learnfrenchlanguageguide.com/learn-french-grammar/asking-yes-no-questions-in-french

Mc Ginty C.

Asking Questions in French: www.thisfrenchlife.com/thisfrenchlife/2005/12/asking_question.html

Zap French

Number and Gender: www.zapfrench.com/French-Lessons/Genre.htm

Interactive whiteboards

BNET, 2007.

I Love My Interactive Whiteboard: http://findarticles.com/p/articles/mi_6950/is_2/ai_n28452816

Inquiry, 2009.

Interactive Whiteboards: www.inquiringmind.co.nz/interactive_whiteboards.htm

Levy, P., 2002.

Interactive Whiteboards in Two Sheffield Schools: A Developmental Study.: http://dis.shef.ac.uk/eirg/projects/wboards.htm

Maddon, Nikki, 2007.

I Love My Interactive Whiteboard: Part II: http://findarticles.com/p/articles/mi_6950/is_2/ai_n28452816

Virtual Learning, 2009.

How Do Interactive Whiteboards Enhance Learning?: www.virtuallearning.org.uk/whiteboards/Learning_theories.pdf

Internet

Cilt, 2009.

Using Wikis to Promote Independent Work in the 14–18 MFL Classroom: www.cilt.org.uk/14to19/ict/wikis/principles.htm

Classroom Resources, 2002.

The Language Teachers Guide to the internet. [Photocopiable]: *www.classroom-resources.co.uk/acatalog/Online_Catalogue_The_Language_Teacher_s_Guide_to_the_Internet_1352.html*

Internet for Foreign Languages, 2009.

Internet for Foreign Languages Home: www.vts.intute.ac.uk/tutorial/modernlanguages

Language learning habits

James, G. 2003. *The Complete Guide to Learning a Language.* Oxford: How to Books Ltd.

Language Learning Tips.

How to Form Positive Habits That Will Help You Reach Your Goal: www.language-learning-tips.com/02_forming_positive_habits.htm

Metz's Japanese Language Learning Clinic, 2009.

Tips on How to Study Japanese Effectively: http://www4.ncsu.edu/~fljpm/clinic/sj11.study.html

Pinker, S., 1999.

The Regular Habits of Language Learning: http://entertainment.timesonline.co.uk/tol/arts_and_entertainment/books/book_extracts/article773282.ece

University of Kent, 2009.

Action Planning: www.kent.ac.uk/careers/sk/skillsactionplanning.htm

Listening

About.com

French Listening Comprehension: http://french.about.com/library/listening/bl-listeningindex.htm

BBC Bitesize

Preparing for the Listening Exam: www.bbc.co.uk/schools/gcsebitesize/french/examskills/1listeningexamrev1.shtml

Bodin

French Foundation Listening: www.teachnet-uk.org.uk/2006%20Projects/MFL-Foundation_Listening/1FoundationListening/Index.htm

Ciel Bretagne

Exercises to Prepare for French Listening: www.ciel.fr/learn-french/comprehension-exercises.htm

Classroom Resources

AQA Interactive Past Listening Papers Higher: www.classroom-resources.co.uk/acatalog/Online_Catalogue_AQA_French_GCSE_Interactive_Past_Papers__Higher_Tier_1248.html

Français Extra

French Listening Exercises: www.francais-extra.co.uk/gateway/listening/listeningindex.htm

Free Language, 2009.

Improve French Listening Skills: http://freelanguage.org/learn-french/skill-enhancement/improve-french-listening-skills

FSL ALL, 2009.

Listening Search: www.fslall.com/learn_french_297.html

GCSE.com, 2009.

Higher Listening: www.gcse.com/french/listening_higher.htm

Listening and Responding Exam: www.gcse.com/french/listening.htm

Radio Time, 2009.

French Radio: http://radiotime.com/genre/c_143/French.aspx

Mindmapping

Buzan World, 2009.

Mindmaps: www.buzanworld.com/Mind_Maps.htm

JCU Study Skills Online, 2009.

Mindmap: www.jcu.edu.au/office/tld/learningskills/mindmap

Mindmap, 2009.

Mindmap: www.mindmap.com

Mindmap Examples, 2009.

Examples: www.mind-mapping.co.uk/mind-maps-examples.htm

Mind-mapping, 2009.

Using Mindmaps Effectively: www.mind-mapping.co.uk/mind-maps-ideas.htm

Russell, P. 2009.

Mindmaps: www.peterrussell.com/MindMaps/mindmap.php

The Thinking Business, 2009.

Mindmaps: www.thethinkingbusiness.co.uk/mind_mapping_create.html

Note-taking

Dover Sherborn Community, 2004.

Making Notes: www.doversherborn.org/doverelementary/Library/CANADA/MakingNotes.htm

Skills 4 Study, 2009.

Making Notes: www.palgrave.com/skills4study/studyskills/reading/notes.asp

Thorns, C., 2005.

Making Notes: http://homepage.ntlworld.com/chris.thorns/skills/making_notes.htm

Past Papers

AQA, 2009.

GCSE French A 3651: http://web.aqa.org.uk/qual/gcse/french_a_assess.php

WJAC/CBAC, 2009. *WJAC/CBAC*

Home: www.wjec.co.uk

Pronunciation

About.com, 2009

French Pronunciation: http://french.about.com/library/pronunciation/bl-pronunciation.htm

French Audio Dictionary: http://french.about.com/library/pronunciation/bl-audiodico.htm

BBC, 2009

French Steps Pronunciation Tips: www.bbc.co.uk/languages/french/lj/pronunciation

Publishing

Blogger, 2009. *Home: www.blogger.com*

Continuum, *www.continuumbooks.com*

Lightningsource.com, 2009. *Home: www.lightningsource.com*

Reading

Arizona Education, 2009.

Online Magazines in French: http://w3.coh.arizona.edu/french/uoa/magazine.html

Authentik, 2009.

Authentik Language Learning Resources: www.authentik.com

BBC Bitesize, 2009.

Preparing for the Reading Exam: www.bbc.co.uk/schools/gcsebitesize/french/examskills/2readingexamrev1.shtml

Brown, J. 2009.

'Why and how textbooks should encourage extensive reading'. *ELT Journal*, 63, pp 238–45.

Classroom resources, 2009.

MFL French Reading Scheme. [Photocopiable]: www.classroom-resources.co.uk/acatalog/Online_Catalogue_MFL_French_Reading_Scheme_1337.html

European Bookstore, 2009.

Catalogue French: www.younglinguists.com/languagebooks/subject/FRE/m4

France 2, 2009.

France 2 Home: www.france2.fr

GCSE.com, 2009

Higher Reading: www.saltgrammar.org.uk/pdf/GCSEFrenchrevision.pdf

Reading and Responding: www.gcse.com/french/reading.htm

Google 2009

Actualités. [Online news]: ttp://news.google.fr

Globegate, 2009.

Reading in French: http://globegate.utm.edu/french/globegate_mirror/reading.html

Holton, F., 2007.

Jacqui et Jacqueline. [Photocopiable]: www.zigzageducation.co.uk/synopses/2420.asp?filename=2420

Lectures de France, 2009.

Reading Practice Test French. [Photocopiable]: http://lecturesdefrance.com/shop/index.php?action=item&id=2211

Linguascope.com, 2009.

Online Catalogue Readers French: http://shop.linguascope.com/acatalog/Readers_French.html

Mary Glasgow Magazines, 2009.

Teenage Subjects for Teenage Language Learners: http://maryglasgowmagazines.com

Pigada, M and Scmitt, N. 2006.

'Vocabulary Acquisition for Extensive Reading: A Case Study'. *Reading in a Foreign Language,* April 18 (1).

Prowse, Philip, 2002.

'Top Ten Principles for Teaching Extensive Reading: A Response'. *Reading in a Foreign Language.* October, 14 (2): *http://nflrc.hawaii.edu/RFL/October2002/discussion/prowse.html*

Revilo, 2009.

Carte Blanche. [Reading Cards]: www.revilolang.com/schools_cards.cfm

Shop Linguascope, 2009.

Catalogue: http://shop.linguascope.com/acatalog/Readers_French.html

Unipresse, 2009.

Youth and Kids Magazines: www.unipresse.com/?gclid=CLrDzc2i9JYCFQECGgodCmLKXQ

Search sites (French)

Amazon France: www.amazon.fr

Google Canada, 2009: www.google.ca/intl/fr

TFI, 2009.

Infos: http://videos.tf1.fr/infos

Yahoo France: http://fr.yahoo.com

Speaking

BBC Bitesize, 2009.

Preparing for the French Exam: www.bbc.co.uk/schools/gcsebitesize/french/examskills/5speakingroleplayrev_print.shtml

Role Play at a Hotel: www.bbc.co.uk/schools/gcsebitesize/french/speakingf/f06_role_hotel_rev1.shtml

Role Play in a Restaurant: www.bbc.co.uk/schools/gcsebitesize/french/speakingh/h03_role_restaurant_rev1.shtml

Preparing for the Speaking Exam: Conversation: www.bbc.co.uk/schools/gcsebitesize/french/examskills/3speakingconversationrev1.shtml

Le Français au Collège, 2009.

French GCSE Role Plays: www.lefrancaisaucollege.co.uk/French_GCSE_Role_plays_English_version.doc

GCSE.com, 2009.

Speaking Exam: www.gcse.com/french/speaking.htm

James, G. 2001.

French Topic Sheets. [Photocopiable]: www.classroom-resources.co.uk/acatalog/Online_Catalogue_French_Topic_Sheets_1347.html

Langweb, 2009.

French GCSE Orals Edexcel: www.langweb.co.uk/GCSEorals/FrenchMenu.htm

Quia, 2009.

GCSE French Role Plays: www.quia.com/ws/334597.html

Seven Kings High School, 2009.

GCSE French Role Plays: http://sevenkingsmfl.typepad.com/gcse_french/c_role_plays

Stationery suppliers

The Consortium, 2009.

Buy School Stationery Online: www.theconsortium.com/school-stationery.htm

Office Shopping, 2009.

Back2School: www.officeshopping.co.uk/features/backtoschool.asp

Staples, 2009.

Office Products Made Easy: www.staples.co.uk/ENG/catalog/stap_home.asp?ct=1

Tandem Learning

Tandem Server Bochum, 2009.

Apprentissage des Langues en Tandem: http://tandem.ac-rouen.fr/learning/idxeng11.html

Town Trials

James, G. 2009.

Berck Plage Tour de Ville: www.bridgehouselanguages.com

Boulogne Tour de Ville: www.bridgehouselanguages.com

Le Touquet Tour de Ville: www.bridgehouselanguages.com

Vocabulary

About.com

French Vocabulary Lessons and Lists: http://french.about.com/od/vocabulary/French_Vocabulary_Lessons_Lists.htm

French Today

French Vocabulary Lessons: www.frenchtoday.com/vocabulary

Peckham, Bob.

Acquiring French Vocabulary: www.utm.edu/staff/globeg/vocab.shtml

Pigada, M and Scmitt, N. 2006.

'Vocabulary Acquisition for Extensive Reading: A Case Study'. *Reading in a Foreign Language,* April 18 (1).

Quiz Tree, 2009.

French Vocabulary: www.utm.edu/staff/globeg/vocab.shtml

Speak French

French Vocabulary: www.speakfrench.co.uk/vocab

Syvum

Learn French Improve Your Vocabulary with Word Games: www.syvum.com/learn/vocabulary/French

Voice Control

Develop Your Voice, 2009.

Develop Your Voice Home: www.developyourvoice.co.uk/index.html

Voice Gym, 2009.

Voice Gym Home: www.voicegym.co.uk

Why learn langauges

Frost's Meditations, 2009.

Why Learn Languages: www.martinfrost.ws/htmlfiles/aug2008/learnlanguage.html

Language Learning Advisor, 2009.

Why Learn Languages: www.language-learning-advisor.com/why-learn-languages.html

Parkway School District, 2009.

Why Learn Languages: www.pkwy.k12.mo.us/C_I/pkwyfl/whylearn.cfm

Writing

About.com, 2009

French Writing Links and Resources: http://french.about.com/od/writing/French_Writing_Links_and_Resources_Write_in_French.htm

BBC Bitesize, 2009.

Checking Your Writing: www.bbc.co.uk/schools/gcsebitesize/french/examskills/9checkingyourwritingrev1.shtml

BBC Bitesize, 2009

Preparing for the Writing Exam: www.bbc.co.uk/schools/gcsebitesize/french/examskills/6writingexamrev1.shtml

GCSE.com, 2009

French Writing Exam: www.gcse.com/french/writing.htm

French Writing Tips: www.gcse.com/french/writing_tips.htm

French Writing Links and Resources – Write in French: http://french.about.com/od/writing/French_Writing_Links_and_Resources_Write_in_French.htm

Appendix 1: How to make a book mark

Here is your template:

Write a haiku in each space:

Roses, les roses chez moi

Comme glaces à la fraise mes joues

En juin, en été

Now centre it

Roses, les roses chez moi

Comme glaces à la fraise mes joues

En juin, en été

Put it in as big a font as possible

Roses, les roses chez moi
Comme glaces à la fraise mes joues
En juin, en été

Print it on to card the same colour as the haiku or in the same colour as the haiku

Roses, les roses chez moi
Comme glaces à la fraise mes joues
En juin, en été

Create a reverse page

Line up all the words you found repeated continuously to cover the whole of an A4 page. If you used a different colour print do the same again or you could go for a similar colour.

Roses, les roses chez moi Comme glaces à la fraise mes joues En juin, en été word word word word word Roses, les roses chez moi Comme glaces à la fraise mes joues En juin, en été word word word word word Roses, les roses chez moi Comme glaces à la fraise mes joues En juin, en été word word word word word Roses, les roses chez moi Comme glaces à la fraise mes joues

Print on to the reverse

If possible, laminate the paper. Don't worry if you can't. Cut out your bookmarks and enjoy!